Library
Western Wyoming Community College

DISCARDED

Women Home Alone

HOW THIS BOOK CAN HELP

The aim of this book is to help women who live or spend a good bit of time alone

- cope with difficulties,
- conquer frustrations, and
- celebrate the possibilities of being alone.

It suggests ways a woman home alone, single or married, can

- make confident decisions,
- overcome loneliness,
- avoid emotional traps,
- build a family team,
- deal with medical emergencies,
- stay safe,
- manage money wisely,
- make minor house and car repairs, and
- build various networks of support.

With this book a Woman Home Alone can learn to thrive!

Women Home Alone

Learning to Thrive

Help for Single Women, Single Moms, Widows,
and Wives Who Are Frequently Alone

PATRICIA H. SPRINKLE

ZondervanPublishingHouse
Grand Rapids, Michigan

A Division of HarperCollinsPublishers

Women Home Alone
Copyright © 1996 by Patricia H. Sprinkle

Requests for information should be addressed to:

▦ ZondervanPublishingHouse
Grand Rapids, Michigan 49530

Library of Congress Cataloging-in-Publication Data

Sprinkle, Patricia Houck.
    Women home alone: learning to thrive / Patricia H. Sprinkle.
      p. cm.
       ISBN: 0-310-20183-7 (softcover)
    1. Wives – Religious life. 2. Wives – Conduct of life. 3. Self-management
(Psychology) 4. Self-help techniques. I. Title.
BV4527.S663 1995
248.8'43-dc 20   95-42134
        CIP

All Scripture quotations, unless otherwise indicated, are taken from the *Holy
Bible: New International Version*®. NIV®. Copyright © 1973, 1978, 1984 by
International Bible Society. Used by permission of Zondervan Publishing House.
All rights reserved.

All rights reserved. No part of this publication may be reproduced, stored in a
retrieval system, or transmitted in any form or by any means—electronic,
mechanical, photocopy, recording, or any other—except for brief quotations in
printed reviews, without the prior permission of the publisher.

Edited by Sandra L. Vander Zicht and Lori J. Walburg
Interior design by Sue Vandenberg Koppenol

Printed in the United States of America

---

96 97 98 99 00 01 02 03 / ❖ DH/ 10 9 8 7 6 5 4 3 2

Dedicated to Paula Rhea,
whose inspiration and scrupulous proofreading enriched this book
almost as much as knowing her enriches me.

CONTENTS

PART THREE
Putting Other People in the Picture

PART FOUR
Money Matters!

PART FIVE
When Faucets Leak and Batteries Die

PART SIX
Learning to Thrive

CHECKLISTS

ACKNOWLEDGMENTS

This book was conceived by Robert and Judy Harris, who sensed God calling me to write on this subject before I did. Thanks to them, and to the women's Bible study who encouraged me to propose this book to the publisher "Because *we* really need it."

I could never have written it without the support and encouragement of many women home alone who agreed to share their experiences and wisdom. I introduce those who gave me formal interviews at the end of the book. There were others, however, whose names I never knew but who, as soon as they heard I was writing the book, contributed one sentence, one anecdote, or one new idea—often on an airplane, at the mirror in a ladies's room, or across the counter while tallying my purchases. Thanks to you, too, for enriching this book immeasurably.

In addition, I owe deep gratitude to several people who helped improve the manuscript out of their special expertise: Dr. Moira Burke, who checked and improved the medical chapter; retired police lieutenant Helen Sweatt, who read and suggested good changes for chapters on security; certified financial planner Mary Lynne McDonald, who improved the financial chapters; and Lawrence Kippenhan, carpenter with Dade County Public Schools, who kept me straight on how to do household repairs. Thanks to Paula Rhea for going over the manuscript with her usual fine-toothed comb. And thanks to Bob and David for putting up with me through the many hours it took to research, write, and revise this manuscript.

Finally, thanks to my editor, Sandra Vander Zicht, who pulls out the best I have to offer and has become more than an editor—a friend.

PREFACE

By the time they reach sixty-five, forty-one percent of all women in the United States live alone! Currently, twenty-six million women head households. Uncounted other women head households while their husbands are away.

But who am I to write a book about and for women home alone? In our family, I am the one who flies away to teach workshops or attend writers' conferences. My husband stays home to feed the bird, get kids off to school, and pay bills on time. I decided to write *Women Home Alone* because I was urged to do so by women who knew of my concern for their situation and needs.

At that point, my only experience as a woman alone for any length of time was twice when Bob had moved early and left me behind until the children finished a school term.

God, however, has a sense of humor.

Less than a month after I signed the contract for this book, Bob was offered a job in another city, and moved early again. This time he left a house that needed a good bit of work before it could be sold, and I had both a writing deadline and a very painful muscle spasm in one hip. For four interminable months I was a woman home alone, limping around papering a kitchen, selling a house, packing, finishing a book, getting the boys through the end of the school year, driving them to summer conferences, and calling movers.

Two years later, as I was finishing the revisions, Bob and the boys left for a couple of weeks again! Therefore, I completed this book as I began it, as a woman home alone.

As a result of my unexpected "lab" experiences, this book is salted with personal anecdotes and insights. Prayers at the beginning of many chapters are from my own journal as I went through periods of challenge, stretching, frustration, and—occasionally—celebration.

To be truly authentic, however, I found that this book—just as my earlier books *Women Who Do Too Much* and *Do I Have To?*—needed the wisdom of experts: women who are regularly home alone. I am grateful to those who granted formal interviews and checked completed chapters. They are introduced at the end of the book.

We did both individual and group interviews, and group dynamics were most exciting. Women recognized wisdom they hadn't realized they had. They also discovered women who shared their aloneness.

In writing this book, I have learned that women are seldom prepared to live alone. Few of us expect to grow up and spend so much time without a man around in times of joy or crisis. I pray that this book will be a help to readers who are women home alone and open the eyes of many others to women home alone in our midst.

P.S. If some readers happen to be men home alone, you are welcome to any help you find in these pages.

PART ONE

*Just You and Me,
God!*

INTRODUCTION

You are not really alone.

Fourteen million women in the U.S.A. live alone.

An additional twelve million women are single mothers.

That's 26,000,000 women home alone or alone with children.[1] Nobody has counted the other women home alone—married women whose husbands are

salesmen	military men	night shift workers
police officers	firefighters	doctors and nurses
pilots	taxi drivers	corporate executives
politicians	athletes	entertainers
truck drivers	in jail	church and mission executives

And then there are the wives of loners—men who may be physically there, but whose wives are socially and emotionally home alone.

The lives of wives alone are much like that of women who are widowed, married, and divorced—with an additional twist: invisibility. Few people know how much they are alone.

Karen, married to an engineer, says ruefully, "It's hard to convince people that my husband is gone as much as he is. When they see him in church almost every Sunday, they aren't aware when he's been gone from Monday until Friday."

The next few chapters deal with issues of isolation: making confident decisions; dealing with worries and loneliness; and being alone for holidays, meals, and medical emergencies. When you finish them, use Checklists 1–3 in the back of the book to make sure you are prepared to be a woman home alone.

CHAPTER ONE

Millions of Courageous Women

Lord, I actually looked forward to my husband's moving early. I counted on reading late at night, cooking easier meals, rocking on the porch with our boys. I did not count on end-of-school madness, a muscle spasm in one hip that makes driving excruciating, or not being able to find leftover paint to touch up the walls. I spent most of today overwhelmed. I don't think I can cope with all this, Lord. If you've got any extra guardian angels, please assign them to us.

This book was born one Sunday morning, just before church. Our pianist, a single woman in her mid-thirties, yawned widely and explained, "I woke up at four thinking I heard a noise in the apartment. I couldn't get back to sleep, of course."

"Haven't you gotten used to being alone by now?" I asked.

She covered another yawn. "You don't ever get used to waking up and wondering if somebody's coming in."

Two minutes later I greeted a woman with five children and deep circles under her eyes. "My husband's out of town for two weeks," she lamented, "and about midnight the baby spiked a high fever. I had to wake everybody and drag them to the hospital. We were in the emergency room half the night."

"Why didn't you call somebody to come stay with the other children while you were at the hospital?" I asked, aghast.

She looked at me as if I were crazy. "Who could I have called at that hour?"

Before I could reply, a divorced mother of three stomped in. "I don't know what I'm going to do about my car! It broke down yesterday on the expressway, and nobody stopped for nearly two hours. I finally got it towed and bought a new battery—which I couldn't afford—and now it's acting up again. How am I supposed to get to work tomorrow if it goes out on me?"

A childless woman in her forties joined us. "How's everything going?" I asked.

She shrugged. "Well, my husband's been out of town all week and was supposed to get back Friday, but now he has to stay in the field until Tuesday." She sounded forlorn.

"You must really miss him," I said sympathetically.

"Yeah," she admitted, "especially this week. Yesterday was my birthday."

As I slipped into my pew, I felt like the beggar who exclaimed, "I once was blind, and now I see!" For the first time, I noticed how many women in our congregation were single, widowed, or divorced, and how many husbands in the congregation were frequently away. Almost within touching distance were a Coast Guard pilot, three members of the Corps of Engineers, a staff member for a mission agency who traveled overseas several times a year, a salesman who traveled a three-state territory for his company, a man who owned his own consulting business and traveled nationwide, and a mother of two whose husband worked long hours and spent the rest of his time on the couch watching television.

How many birthdays, medical emergencies, nighttime scares, and auto breakdowns did women in our congregation face alone?

Over the next few weeks I began to notice so many women home alone that I began to wonder: "Am I the only woman in the world whose husband comes home regularly almost every night?"

Some time later, I asked a Bible study to pray about what book I should write next. One woman said without hesitation, "My husband and I were talking just this week. We think you ought to write a book for women home alone. You have a real burden for us."

With the word *us*, she swept her hand around the table. In that group of eight, two were single, one was divorced, two had husbands who traveled, one was married to a Coast Guard pilot, and one was married to a man who played with a Christian band out of town most weekends. I was stunned to realize that in my own Bible study group, I *was* the only woman who wasn't frequently home alone!

YOU ARE NOT ALONE

Single, widowed, divorced, or married, women home alone have many of the same problems:

1. Isolation. Nobody is there in times of crisis. Equally, nobody is around to share little joys and understand special moments. Judi, a widow, says, "I go for days without talking to anybody except the cat. I find myself talking to strangers in the supermarket."

This isolation is intensified for married women home alone. While single, divorced, or widowed women may seek one another out, married women are alone erratically and "hate to bother" other women. Many can't even name other married acquaintances who are frequently alone. One satisfying part of interviewing for this book was watching these women begin to notice one another.

2. Inconvenience. Allison, whose husband travels weekly in sales, says with a sigh, "If I can't find something, I have to wait until he calls so I can ask him." Barbara Holland writes, "It's inconvenient, this solitary life. Nobody lends a hand. We can't say, 'Would you get the door for me?—hand me the towel?—hold up the other end?—go see what's making that funny noise?—grab the cat while I shove the pill down her?—answer the phone?—mail a letter?—put your finger on this knot?'"[2]

3. Indecision. "Most of all, I hate having to make all the decisions," says Sarah Gay, a single teacher. Trained by society that financial matters and home/auto maintenance are "men's business," women home alone have to decide how to invest money, what to repair, and what to replace. They have to decide when a child is sick enough to take to the doctor, and whom to call in an emergency.

4. Lack of respect. Decision making is complicated by a lack of respect from mechanics, contractors, bankers, salespersons, doctors, and other "authorities." The Jacksonville *Florida Times Union* reported in 1994 that "Demographically, about thirty percent of the homes in Duval and four surrounding counties are headed by single people with no relatives living with them. A family of one. On a day-to-day basis, some of these singles say they deal with a world skewed toward couples and families. Sometimes the societal predisposition to favor couples is obvious. More often, though, it is a prejudice of subtleties and perceptions."[3]

A divorced woman I met briefly on a plane said bitterly, "If I'd known how much of a hassle I'd get from building contractors, I'd never have tried to remodel my home."

5. Loneliness. Loneliness is one of the hardest parts of being alone. Mothers at home with preschoolers suffer it as intensely as women without children. Jane pointed out a special problem for the recently divorced: "After the divorce I didn't have the same friends. With widows, there are no sides to take. With divorced friends, people think they have to be his friend or her friend."

Faith and prayer help with loneliness, but do not automatically keep women from being lonely, afraid, and overwhelmed when they have to live or stay alone for extended periods of time.

6. Burnout. Almost every woman home alone comes to a frightening point where she feels overwhelmed by having primary responsibility for her financial, social, and domestic life. This is very hard on women who have envisioned a future shared with a strong mate.

Among women I interviewed, widows seemed to have less burnout than other women home alone. Jean gives a clue why that might be true. "I have two sisters, one widowed and one divorced. Everybody pitched in to help the widowed sister, but people didn't know what to say to the divorced one. Also, the widowed one got insurance money. The divorced one did not."

However, any woman home alone has to do all the cooking, cleaning, repairs, driving, and child care—and often hold down a job as well. No wonder so many admit "I'm just worn out."

BENEFITS THEY SHARE

Just as they share certain problems, women home alone have some advantages over women with husbands at home:

1. Freedom. Women home alone can curl up with a good book instead of fixing dinner, read late at night, go to bed early, decide what to eat and when, spread craft projects all over the house, or stay out late with friends. They can be neat or messy, loud or quiet, well dressed or slobs. Nobody complains. Who even sees?

Women with children, of course, have more restrictions on their freedom, but they admit, "I like making the rules without consulting somebody else."

2. More time for prayer. "When my husband is traveling," Judy says, "we both get more time to pray. We have the time we'd usually be spending with one another."

3. More time for others. "If my husband weren't gone so much," says Allison, "I'd never be able to do everything I do in our church. I'd want to spend that time with him."

4. Friendships. Many women home alone have built strong support groups with other women. They meet for meals, go to movies together, or just rock on a porch and sip iced tea. Women who discover the joy of being with other women seldom feel quite so alone.

NEEDED: A NEW DEFINITION OF ALONENESS

Before a woman home alone can celebrate her situation, she may need a new definition of what it means to be alone. Stephen M. Johnson, author of *First Person Singular,* urges people alone to move toward what he calls "autonomous adulthood," which, he says, requires the mastery of two skills:

- how to acquire and maintain a well-operating social support group, and

- how to perform all self-care functions that married people may generally share.[4]

In the following chapters we shall consider both. What Johnson calls "self-care functions" are really a complete "job description" for living alone that includes:

cooking	housekeeping
transportation	house maintenance
car maintenance	health maintenance
managing money	child care
staying safe	making/keeping friends

developing personal interests and hobbies

building a database of persons on whom to call in various types of emergencies

This book can help a woman home alone acquire skills she does not currently have, giving her confidence in her ability to thrive.

A WISE WOMAN KNOWS
*Living alone is a challenge
with much to be learned,
not a discomfort to be endured.*

IN CONCLUSION

Millions of women spend much of their time home alone. They can find it overwhelming, or they can take steps to learn to thrive in that situation. Living alone may be considered as a job, for which a person must prepare. As you read the following chapters, set goals to master new skills you need. Read some of the suggested books for further reading, and use the checklists at the end of the book to help you get and stay prepared for emergencies. *Look now at Checklist 1, "Woman Home Alone Preparedness Kit," to see how prepared you already are.*

Then let's consider a prime issue for all women home alone: how to make major decisions with confidence.

Suggested Further Reading

Freudenberger, Dr. Herbert J., and Gail North. *Women's Burnout: How to Spot It, How to Reverse It, and How to Prevent It.* New York: Doubleday, 1985. A good book to read before you get burned out, but helpful afterwards, too.

Holland, Barbara. *One's Company: Reflections on Living Alone.* New York: Ballantine, 1992. Humorous, honest, insightful, and wise!

CHAPTER TWO

In the Valley of Decision

Lord, a bloody stream of water is oozing from my freezer. Why did it have to die on a hot June day, full of meat? Can it be fixed, or do I need a new one? Whom can I call whose opinion I can trust? And if I have to buy a new freezer alone, can I really do it? I don't want to make an expensive mistake. God, of all the parts I hate about being on my own, I most hate having to make all the decisions.

One of the primary skills a woman home alone must learn is to make confident decisions. That's tough! Helplessness has been held up for generations as a feminine virtue. Aren't we supposed to teeter uncertainly on the brink of a crisis until a strong man comes to our rescue? Even women who are basically independent often let a man shoulder tough decisions if he will. And some women are delighted to let a man—any man—make all the decisions.

A friend who recently lost her father told me, "Until Dad died, Mother never wrote a check, never drove a car, never made an important decision. Being a widow has been an enormous adjustment—even beyond her grief over losing Dad."

Women accustomed to making only simple decisions may become paralyzed when expected to make major ones. In *Multiple Choices*, an excellent guide on wise decision making, Ruth Tucker names several kinds of choices women face: impossible, enduring, spiritual, liberating, foolish, manipulative, painful, compromising, confrontational, and compassionate choices. She declares,

> Deciding what to do about the minor choices in life will not automatically prepare us for the major ones.... If we confine ourselves—or let ourselves be confined—to the inconsequential, we neglect our God-given responsibilities and discard our decision-making capabilities by default.[1]

In contrast, making major decisions leads women to the place where we care what others think, but don't depend on them for approval.

A WISE WOMAN KNOWS
Adults ask opinions, not permission.

Of course, it is often nicer to make decisions in consultation with someone else. Doreen, divorced, says, "One of my biggest problems is not having anybody to help me make decisions. How big should the tip be? Would this couch look good in our living room? I have to learn to have faith in my ability to decide." With a twinkle, she adds, "The other side of that, of course, is that there's nobody around saying, 'I told you that wouldn't work,' or 'Why did you pick that color?'"

Wives home alone may defer decisions until a spouse gets home. Lori's husband was away for six months, during which their daughter was born. She remembers, "He wanted me to buy a video camera for the baby, but I didn't want to buy it, because I knew it wouldn't be the one he would want or buy. I told him if he had an idea of what he wanted I'd get it, but otherwise I'd spend two weeks trying to make everybody happy and I still wouldn't. Decision making is so hard when you are obligated to think about somebody else's point of view."

Yet sometimes a decision is inevitable. When there's nobody around to help, here are principles that can help a woman home alone make confident decisions.

SEVEN PRINCIPLES OF MAKING CONFIDENT DECISIONS

1. Decision making is a normal part of life. Making solo decisions for the first time is always hard, particularly for a Christian woman taught that a man is supposed to be a woman's "head" and "covering." When no man is around to make the big decisions, she can become baffled and angry. Where is that head her household is supposed to have? Absent.

She faces the same reality as Naomi in Moab, Esther in Persia, Tamar at the crossroads, and Mary Magdalene on Easter morning: sometimes a woman has to make decisions all by herself and pray she makes the right ones. However . . .

2. Making confident decisions is also a learned skill. We all learn to make decisions by practice. Children who are encouraged to make decisions from early years are more likely to grow up confident of their adult decisions. If men seem more confident about making decisions than women, consider how much more practice they've had! The more decisions you make on your own, the more confident you will get about making them, too.

A WISE WOMAN KNOWS
*Making a good decision is seldom
as hard as believing you can make one.*

Of course, a sad fact of life in our society is that a woman alone simply doesn't command the same respect as a couple or a man alone in many situations. A woman home alone may need to be more assertive when asking for a good restaurant table, turning down unnecessary car and home repairs, and persuading a carpenter to hang her kitchen cabinets so she can reach the top shelves.

Other decisions will involve research in unfamiliar territory. Later chapters will suggest resources to help make wise decisions about house or automobile repairs, financial matters, security, and health concerns. Don't be nervous. If other people can learn about those topics, you can too.

3. Making good decisions is a habit. Look around you and what do you see? People in the habit of making good decisions tend to continue to make good decisions; people in the habit of making poor decisions are apt to continue to make poor ones.

If you have a history of making no decisions, bravely make a few and evaluate: Were they wise? Why or why not? What do I wish I had done differently? In male-dominated areas of life, you may want to use a Male Yardstick: "If my husband/father/brother had to make this decision, what would he be likely to do?" That may help you talk firmly with mechanics and building contractors. Gradually, to your surprise, you will discover you have begun to make wise decisions on your own.

If you have a history of making poor decisions, choose someone who you feel makes good decisions and ask her or him to help you with your next ones. Afterwards, consider the outcomes. Were those wiser decisions than you have been in the habit of making? If so, what made them wiser? Develop a gradual history of making better choices until you are making wise ones habitually.

Often poor decisions are the result of

- ignorance: failing to do the research before making a decision;
- neediness: "I'll do this to show I love myself, because nobody else does";
- impulse: decision making without considering consequences; or
- magical thinking: "I'll go ahead and do this, and a fairy godmother, lottery ticket, new man, or miracle will turn up to rescue me from the consequences."

Knowing why you make poor decisions can be a first step toward beginning to make wiser ones.

4. Decisions should move you toward long-range goals. A woman I know was once a tightrope walker in the Florida State University Circus. "How did you keep from falling?" I asked.

"Just keep your eye on where you want to go," she replied.

As women, we live our lives in seasons—time periods framed by events such as "while I keep this job," "until I retire," "as long as my children are in school," "until my husband stops traveling." In *Women Who Do Too Much* (Zondervan, 1991), I discuss how important it is for a woman to define her current season, and I tell how to set goals for that season in all areas of life: personal, professional, family, church, and community. A woman home alone particularly needs to set goals for each season so decisions move her toward where she wants to be.

5. It's all right to ask for help when you need it. Just because a woman is alone, she needn't make all her decisions in a vacuum. Don't risk making a foolish decision because you don't want people to think you're too dumb to make the decision by yourself!

"When I first thought about buying a house," said Sarah Gay, "I asked everybody. We talked about it in the teacher's lunchroom and at choir practice. I needed all the wisdom I could get."

Whereas asking people to make a decision for you helps you avoid decisions, asking them to share their wisdom helps you make your own. If you have a new decision to make, seek wise help. On the other hand, as you get more experienced in decision making, dare to make a few serious decisions yourself. It's thrilling to discover how wise you can be!

6. Wrong decisions are seldom irreversible. Many women get paralyzed by the fear of making a wrong decision. "We are often tempted to simplify the issues and see everything in black and white," declares Ruth Tucker.[2] But life is complex. Decisions are often not between good and bad, right and wrong, but between unpleasant and equally unpleasant, good and equally good. A woman who waits to make a perfect decision may miss an important point:

> The ultimate goal in making right decisions is not to find the will of God, but to do the will of God: to have a sense that our lives have a purpose, and that in the end the Lord will say, "Well done, good and faithful servant!" . . . Our confidence in decision making must grow out of the inner certainty that we are operating on the strength of the Lord.[3]

28

And even when we fail, we have enriched our range of experience. Now we know some things we didn't know before.

7. *Don't sweat the small stuff.* If you have trouble making even small decisions, maybe you aren't asking the right question. Ask yourself, "What do I really want?" For instance, if you spend ages deciding "Would I rather have chicken pot pie or tuna casserole tonight?" maybe what you really want is not to have to make so many nonessential decisions! If you really don't want to decide about some things, don't. Close your eyes and pull a microwave dinner out of the freezer. Don't waste life making decisions you won't remember in a year. As Jesus told one crowd: "Don't be anxious about what you are going to eat or wear."

Save your decision making for something that matters to you.

IN CONCLUSION

If you are a woman home alone, you are going to have to make decisions. Some will be minor, some major. Some will be terrifying. Others will require timid advances into unknown territory to gain knowledge you'd rather not have. You may often wonder if you are making the right decision. However, as Genevieve Davis Ginsberg assures widows, "Ambivalence is not a sign of mental deterioration, it is not an unspeakable social disease. It is perfectly normal to feel insecure about suddenly being in charge after years of team playing."[4] It is equally normal to feel insecure about being in charge after being raised to share decision making.

Take heart! Once you begin to make decisions and see they are wise, you will begin to feel more confident about making them. You will cease to be paralyzed by the fear of making imperfect ones. You will accept that some decisions will inevitably be wrong, but few are irreversible. As your decisions become wiser, you will gain confidence and begin to make them more easily. One day you will wonder why you ever expected a man to make decisions for you!

Women home alone warn, however, that learning to make confident decisions can lead to problems of its own. Frances admits, "When you get to make all the decisions, you can develop a

29

tendency toward selfishness. You get so used to doing what you want when you want to do it."

"And it's easy to get undisciplined," added Paula. "I don't have to be accountable to anybody—spiritually, physically, or mentally. I also lose my adaptability, because I get used to doing things my way."

Well, you've been warned. But don't let that keep you from learning to make confident decisions.

Meanwhile, there are other issues you face—such as worries that keep you awake at night. Let's take a look at worry.

Suggested Further Reading

Sprinkle, Patricia H. *Women Who Do Too Much: Stress and the Myth of the Superwoman*. Grand Rapids: Zondervan, 1991. Helps women set goals for a season and objectives to accomplish those goals.

Tucker, Ruth A. *Multiple Choices: Making Wise Decisions in a Complicated World*. Grand Rapids: Zondervan, 1992. The title says it!

CHAPTER THREE

Keeping Worries Down to Size

*"Lord, give me the serenity to accept the things I cannot change,
the courage to change the things I can,
and the wisdom to know the difference."*

The Serenity Prayer

That's a good prayer for women home alone. It can help cut down on worrying. I'm not talking about the normal kind of worrying that leads to wisdom, such as worrying enough about security to put locks on doors or worrying enough about our health to find a doctor. I'm talking about the kind of anxiety that makes us lie wide-eyed and tense in the night.

Of course, women home alone have so much to worry about! Burglars. Car and household emergencies. Sickness. Losing a job. Paula and Diane worry about having enough money to retire on. Frances, already retired, wonders if her money will hold out for the rest of her life. "I hate to pinch pennies," she admits.

Sarah Gay worries about the future: "What will it be like if I am completely alone in my old age without immediate contacts or support?" Frances's worries along that line are slightly different: "I

31

probably won't be able to live independently forever. I enjoy the life I have, and in the future I'll have to make some changes and decide what they will be."

Even weather can cause a woman home alone to worry. One night Lori's area had tornado warnings. "I'd never felt anything like that! First it was still, then an enormous gust of wind. I worried, 'What am I going to do here by myself with this tiny baby?'"

Coast Guard, Navy, or airline wives worry about ships going down or planes crashing. Lynn, Jill, and Teale worry about their husbands when they travel overseas and cannot call home. Lynn remembers, "Bas was in El Salvador during the civil war and had to travel by bulletproof automobile or helicopter. He was in Mozambique for a month during a civil war there. Guerrillas had often just left the village before Bas and the staff got there. That is the hardest thing for me about being alone: not knowing if he is okay or not. My faith gets stretched farther than it's ever been."

In addition to specific worries, however, it's easy when home alone to just worry in general. "What if?" can become a constant companion, and instead of "what if" being a bridge to wonderful possibilities, most of the "what if's" are terrifying. Remember the old adage, "A coward dies a thousand times, a brave [wo]man only once?" The reason the coward dies so often is that she carefully rehearses every possible fatal alternative!

That kind of worry doesn't make us wiser and better able to cope. Instead, it makes us so afraid we become rigid, reducing our world and simplifying our situation, hoping to control it. Trying to shove back the dark edges of worry, women may engage in compulsive orgies of housecleaning, overeating, exercise, or oversleeping. Some stay too busy for friends, or bury themselves in work. All of those increase stress and lead to burnout.

Priscilla described her own situation after her divorce several years ago. "I allowed work to overtake me so much that I didn't enjoy the good parts of being alone. Being home was just a grind of getting the laundry done and surviving."

Obviously, if worry increases terror, stress, and burnout, it needs to go. But how?

FIVE WAYS TO CUT DOWN ON WORRY

1. Concentrate on today. Doreen said, "I used to worry about everything, until my counselor taught me that I only have to deal with today's problems. Don't borrow problems from the past or future. Build on the past, plan for the future, but live for today. When I get worried about something, I try to ask myself, 'Is this something I have to deal with *today*?' If not, I leave off worrying about it until it's time to deal with it."

2. Stick to your own worries. We can get so enmeshed in worries about others—our children, our parents, our coworkers, our friends—that we have little energy for our own lives. Doreen's counselor also taught her to ask the same question with the emphasis on the personal pronoun: "Is this something *I* have to deal with today?"

3. Give God worries you can do nothing about. For a time, Doreen kept a large paper bag she had labeled "God's bag." "When I was worried about something I couldn't seem to do anything about, I wrote it down on a card and put it in God's bag. I dealt with what I could, and let God worry about the rest. For me, that worked. I needed something physically concrete for a time until I got in the habit of turning my worries over to God."

A WISE WOMAN KNOWS
*Some problems cannot be solved,
but you can make peace with them.*

4. Stabilize yourself with daily devotions and exercise. Jill, who also tends to be a worrier, says, "I find that daily devotions stabilize me. If I have my devotions and go for a walk, I worry less."

5. Instead of worrying, plan and solve. "Worry is a drab double of a dream, a dream in its least imaginative form."[1] Worry seldom leads to planning, and almost never to solutions. Instead of worrying, pick one area of life where you feel particularly dissatisfied, helpless, or stuck, and write down what you want in that area.

Then, think of one thing you can do toward providing what you want. It may be a small thing. If you want a prettier home, you can buy one pretty item, or paint one room. If you want to look better, you can get a better haircut or throw out all the clothes you hate and wear only those that make you feel good. If you want a better job, you can take career counseling to see what you are good at, improve a skill, read want ads, or talk to friends who may have contacts in an area you'd rather be in.

This is not a quick process; it takes time. But instead of worrying about a situation, take a baby step toward getting what you want.

IN CONCLUSION

Worry accomplishes nothing, and leaves us feeling wrung out, exhausted, and fearful. Taking a hard look at your worries can be the first step toward deciding which need to be turned over to God and which offer you a problem that can be solved.

And since one ongoing worry for many women home alone is loneliness, let's look at that next.

Suggested Further Reading

Matthew 6:25–34 and Psalm 37.

CHAPTER FOUR

Even My Shadow Is Lonely

Lord, why have you given a full moon to flood my porch swing tonight and the scent of gardenias on the breeze, and failed to provide somebody to enjoy them with? I feel not only unloved, but unlovable, and find my own company about as exciting as dust balls.

At some point, most women home alone have to deal with loneliness. Loneliness is not the same as aloneness. Aloneness is when we are by ourselves and having a pleasant time. Loneliness is a gray, gnawing thing of the heart that chills our spirit and saps our energy.

Dot spoke of the months after her husband died. "I hated getting in that bed alone, waking up in the night, and not hearing him breathe. Even not smelling him there! I used to splash some of his cologne on the extra pillow."

Loneliness comes in many forms. It can be caused by too much aloneness, and may spur us back into the stream of life, or it can creep up on us in a crowd. It can overtake us if we've been doing too much for others without finding support for ourselves. Some of the loneliest women in the world are married to loners who are home every night, but emotionally in a world of their own.

35

Loneliness is embarrassing to admit, because solitude is so highly extolled. As Barbara Holland wryly notes, "Here we are, alone because nobody wants us, and lonely because we're so spineless and empty-headed we can't find inspiration in our solitude."[1]

How can a woman home alone deal with loneliness?

IT'S OKAY TO BE MISERABLE

Remember the old childish song: "Nobody loves me, everybody hates me, I'm going to eat some worms"? When we're lonely, a little person deep inside us whimpers, "I don't come first with anybody!"

August said, "When my husband's gone, I hate to see other couples having fun, and it's hard for me to get up the gumption to go do something by myself even if I can find a sitter. When I'm lonely, it's easy to think, 'Everybody's got somebody except me.'"

At that point, instead of rushing to fill the vacuum, maybe we should give ourselves permission to be lonely. Put on some favorite music—the kind that puts a lump in the throat—and listen until tears flow. It's okay to cry. We feel miserable because we are!

If loneliness and misery come out in anger, that is also appropriate. It really *isn't* fair that we should be so lonely. However, because anger causes tense muscles, headaches, and ulcers, it's healthier to work through that anger and get rid of it—push ourselves into activity that can help release it: play the piano, attack messy closets, go for a walk or a run or a bike ride, pound pillows, throw rocks. When we wear out our body, our spirit can relax and admit that it is deeply, truly sad.

One author recommends, "The basic way out of loneliness is not to go around it or climb over it, not to escape from it or bottle it up . . . but to face it squarely, analyzing it, understanding it . . . and finally making it your friend."[2]

The next time you feel lonely, accept that loneliness. Sit quietly and feel just how lonely you are.

PUT THE LONELINESS TO USE

Obviously, it's not healthy to stay lonely forever. Loneliness wallows so happily in self-pity! Therefore, once we have admitted

36

that we are lonely and it's not fair—which is one way of admitting that we are, after all, lovable—what then? Here are a few ideas:

1. Analyze what makes you most lonely and steer clear of that. Lori says, "When I'm feeling a little lonely and I'm in the house with his stuff all over the place, it makes me lonelier than ever, so I have learned to get out of the house and take a drive. I go to the beach where it's pretty and I can sit and think a bit, then I tend to get over it."

2. Consciously replace negative thoughts with positive ones. In loneliness, our negative tapes play loudly: "I'm never going to . . .," "I can't . . .," "I wish . . ." Those thoughts only make us more depressed and lonely. Deliberately replace "I'll never succeed" with "I have what it takes to succeed." Replace "I'm lazy" with "I have energy to do what I want to do." Replace "I wish" with "I'm going to take steps to make my dreams come true." Replace "I wish I didn't always have to go alone" with "I am going somewhere I choose to go, with people I enjoy being with."

3. Use loneliness to get better acquainted with yourself. Loneliness is not pleasant, but it can be useful. Loneliness and depression have been identified as the final stage of grief. Out of loneliness, our spirits rise up and cry, "Enough!" Therefore, well-meaning friends do a grieving woman no favor by making sure she is never alone.

Equally important, loneliness provides solitude. Anthony Storr, clinical lecturer in psychiatry at Oxford University, claims that solitude is essential if the brain is to function at its best and if we are to fulfill our highest potential. In this high-tech world, we easily become separated from our deepest needs and feelings. Solitude provides space to learn, think, create, and maintain contact with our own inner world.[3]

A WISE WOMAN KNOWS
*Daydreams are the silver threads
reality is spun from.*

The next time you feel lonely, ask the silence within you:

- Who am I when I'm not with other people?
- What do I enjoy doing when I don't have to take other people's preferences into account?

- What have I stopped doing that I enjoyed in the past?
- What do I like to read when I am not impressing anybody?
- Where do I want to be a few years from now? What will I need to do to get there?
- What would I like to do or be that I haven't tried?

Write down your answers. You may find loneliness spurs you to become more of who you most deeply want to become!

4. *"Turn your loneliness into solitude and your solitude into prayer."*[4] Loneliness can also spur us to get in touch with One who is infinitely great, infinitely caring, and infinitely there. Psalm 46:10 urges: "Be still and know that I am God." Judy says, "When my husband is away, I have so much more time for prayer. And when I truly pray, I no longer am lonely."

MOVE BEYOND LONELINESS

Loneliness saps our energy, but if we are not to become seriously mentally ill, eventually we must get off our duffs and take steps out of loneliness. If "taking steps" sounds too exhausting, remember the Chinese proverb: "A journey of a thousand miles begins with a single step." Here are twelve "first steps" out of the Exhausting Quagmire of Loneliness. No one will or could do all of them. Which most appeal to you?

1. *Do something that shows you care about yourself.* Doing little things to boost ourselves can change both the way we perceive ourselves and the way others perceive us. One counselor tells of a client who was swamped by responsibilities, bills, and unhappiness. One thing she had always wanted was a lovely bed, so the counselor suggested she buy one pillow to represent the better life she was someday going to have. Gradually she added other pillows. As she did, her self-esteem grew. Eventually, she became so self-confident and lovely that she became a model![5]

2. *Make your house your home.* Your living space should not only welcome others, it should also welcome you. Decorate with things that mean something to you. Keep foods on hand that make you feel good. (Did you know that chocolate releases endorphins in women's brains and makes them happier?) Use scents and colors that cheer and refresh you. Buy a canary to sing in your window.

A man wrote about living alone after his divorce: "I never furnished my first apartment, never unpacked the boxes of books and personal belongings ... never entertained in it. My eating habits consisted of ... crackers, cheese, hastily opened cans of soup, and milk, or 'dropping by' my friends' houses just at mealtimes."[6] Sound familiar?

Priscilla confided, "In my marriage I spent my life pleasing others. I'm now learning how to do things to please myself. Last weekend I bought flowers and planted them around my new apartment patio. They are beautiful!" She beamed. "And to think, I planted them just for my own pleasure."

3. PLAN *to fill your time.* When days stretch out in dreary monotony, take charge of your life. Make a plan for tomorrow and this week. Plans don't have to be complicated, but they give structure and purpose to a day—and make you feel accomplished when the day is done.

A WISE WOMAN KNOWS
My direction and fulfillment do not have to come from outside.

If you don't have the energy even to plan to plan, here are some ideas to start with. Make plans to

- invite someone in for a simple, casual meal;
- browse the new book shelf of the library and read one that looks intriguing;
- clean out files or closets;
- bring photo albums up-to-date;
- cook and freeze your favorite meals in one-person portions;
- plant flowers for yourself!

4. *Do something you've always wanted to do—or something utterly new!* One antidote to loneliness is "true involvement in something to the point that you forget all about yourself, your

health, your marital status, your . . . feelings of anxiety and—
especially—what is going to happen next."[7]

"Life with a Loner," an article in *The Washington Post*, urged
women to make a life of their own, pursue their own interests and
develop hobbies.[8] That's because interests can be a great resource
against loneliness if we develop and exercise them. They may even
develop into a passion.

A friend of mine whose husband's law practice often leaves
her home alone always enjoyed "playing in the dirt." When she
heard that local floral shows could use workers, she volunteered.
"Accepting entries for the shows tuned me in to botanical names,"
she says. "I discovered how much there was to learn about plants."
Her interest sparked, she attended a big European floral event and
a state symposium on horticulture. Then she and a friend began
taking horticulture classes at a nearby university. Eventually she
became active in statewide horticulture societies and was invited to
serve on a committee to oversee extensive gardens for a historical
society—all because she followed her joy in "playing in the dirt."

If you need a new interest, might you like to

- learn more about growing plants?
- learn to paint, draw, throw pots, do interior design?
- learn to write stories, poem, or articles?
- take a gourmet cooking class? (A cheap way to eat!)
- begin a collection?
- join a chorus or community orchestra?
- learn to play a new instrument?
- join a community theater group: act, paint scenery,
  make costumes, sell tickets, or prompt the actors?
- volunteer to usher at symphony or theater?
- take up golf, bowling, tennis, swimming, hockey,
  skiing, scuba diving, or roller blading?
- attend lectures at a local college or museum?
- trace your family genealogy?
- find other women home alone who like to play cards?
- check newspapers for events free to the public?

- collect investment information and attend investment seminars?

Try various things until you find one you like. Even then, you don't have to make a lifelong commitment. Just don't limp along as many women do, developing none of their own interests except those of the men in their lives. Those women think they become interesting by cloning themselves to a man's interests, but that seldom works. What interesting man wants to marry his clone?

A WISE WOMAN KNOWS
Doing what really interests me
makes me more interesting
to everybody—including me.

5. Get a job. Professional work takes the edge off loneliness. June said, "Working makes it easier to have things to think about when he's gone. It also gives me other adults to talk with and be interested in. I don't get lonely very much."

Other working women agreed. "Between work, my children, the house, and church, I really don't have time to be lonely."

6. Get creative! Creative imagination can solace lonely spirits. It can even heal. Renowned Kansan artist Elizabeth Layton, a manic depressive, credited her cure to learning to draw.

Creativity gives us control over part of life. We are not helpless when we are making something. And remember, creativity extends not only to the "fine arts"—music, painting, drawing, writing, dance—but also to crafts: origami, sewing, making colorful hair bows, weaving, recycling objects into new uses.

7. Seek joy! Make joyful times happen. Invite others over to make music, dance, sing, or play games together. Rock needy babies in a hospital nursery. Throw instant parties you don't clean for. When single and living alone, I used to have a party every Friday night. Friends came if they had nothing else to do, to play cards. We drank Cokes, ate popcorn, and laughed ourselves silly.

What do you do for sheer, unadulterated joy?

8. *Get yourself a pet.* Not everybody likes pets, but Suzanne said, "We have four cats and two dogs, and they are my friends. Kids need something to cuddle, and so do I."

Sarah Gay agreed. "Having two cats to take care of is good. And their physical presence beside me on the bed at night or there to keep me company helped ease my grief when my brother died."

9. *Keep a diary or prayer journal.* For some people, writing is almost the same as talking to someone else. If that is true for you and you feel lonely, make your journal a friend.

10. *Exercise.* Exercise is a good low-mood pickup. Physiologically it stimulates respiration and circulation, which makes us feel better. It also focuses our attention on something (aching muscles, sore feet) besides ourselves. When lonely, go for a walk, jog, swim, do yard work, attend a dance or aerobics class, play on a softball or baseball team or a bowling league, or take lessons in some sport you have never mastered.

11. *Talk to yourself.* No matter what you've heard about people who talk to themselves, most women home alone admit they do. As Barbara Holland says, "The condition of loneliness ebbs and flows, . . . but needing to talk goes on forever. It's more basic than needing to listen. . . . The daily small change of complaints and observations and opinions . . . backs up and chokes us. We can't really call a friend to say we got our feet wet walking home, or it's getting dark earlier now, or we don't trust that new Supreme Court Justice."[9]

Don't just talk, but tell yourself jokes or make funny comments about what's going on. Laughter—even alone—is a great healer.

12. *Don't be afraid to have fun alone.* Have you discovered how much fun it can be to travel alone? I find I am far more likely to engage in conversation with others along the way, and I amble through museums or art galleries at my own pace, change plans spontaneously, see what I want to see, and eat when I want to eat—reading a book at the table if I like. I have found people welcome me into their lives far more easily when I am alone.

Sarah Gay goes to movies alone. "It felt funny at first, but now I don't mind. I also didn't like to go to a restaurant alone, because I wondered what other people were thinking. Finally I told myself, 'Look, you aren't thinking weird things about other people who are here alone. Why do you think they are thinking weird things about you?'"

SEEK OTHER PEOPLE

While knowing how to be alone is important, other people are also important. As I interviewed women home alone, I was struck again and again by how often a lonely woman was convinced she was the only one in her particular situation—that everybody else was having fun with others. Lauren pointed out how silly that is. "I think weekends ought to be family time, so when he's not there, I hate to call anybody else. I always think they are having family time. Yet often I call someone on Monday and she says, 'I sat home all day Saturday wishing somebody would call.'"

Several ways women home alone can stay in touch with others:

1. *Actively cultivate friendships.* One of the best antidotes for loneliness is to develop deep, caring, and sympathetic friendships—especially with other women. Women friends offer advantages husbands and male friends do not: they like salad lunches; can talk politics, sports, and theology, but don't mind if the conversation rambles into hairstyles, female health, children, other people, and clothes; seldom stop a conversation to check a football score; don't insist that you eat spicy food just because *they* like it; don't care if you haven't put on mascara or pantyhose; and don't mind if you cry. They even know how to be silly. Suzanne said, "I have one friend who is also a mother alone. We call each other and say, 'This is your Are-you-alive? call.' Then we stay on the phone and giggle for hours."

A WISE WOMAN KNOWS
A faithful friend is a strong defense:
and she who has found one has found a treasure.

Friendships, however, require maintenance. To be a friend we need to remember birthdays and special occasions, watch for signs of depression, and actively seek any who are becoming recluses.

Women home alone have more time to maintain friendships than women busy with husbands and families. Teale said, "When my husband is away, I talk on the phone a lot. My sister and I have become especially close. Also, if he's out of town, I don't have to rush out the door after school. I tend to stand around and talk with other teachers more."

2. Find others who enjoy what you enjoy. If you don't have close friends:

- Get better acquainted with someone who has only been a work "contact" or a church "acquaintance."
- Invite someone you used to know and like to lunch.
- Form an eating club or gourmet society, either cooking for one another or all going out together.
- Invite several other people alone to join you after church for a Dutch treat inexpensive lunch.

When my father took a new job, Mother was left alone several days each week. Retired and living in a new area, she decided to revive a long-neglected flair for art. She took a painting class, then got permission to invite the instructor to begin teaching in her own church. Women she knew slightly in the church began to come, and as they painted together, they became friends.

Places to meet women you might enjoy getting to know better:

community school classes	theater groups
political campaigns	literacy programs
building houses	church school
children's sports	parents' meetings
community choruses	church committees
sports teams	volunteering

3. Travel with other women. My friend who got so heavily involved in botany now takes an annual tour of gardens with other women friends. Sarah Gay and friends took a bicycle tour of bed-and-breakfast inns one summer, and a "rain forest" ecology vacation in Costa Rica another year. Paula and three friends ski each winter. Frances and Doreen went on Alaskan cruises with friends. Allison reports, "My children and I have gone camping with another woman and her children. We camped for a week—two mothers and six children. Were we crazy? Probably. But we had a lot of fun."

4. Seek others who are different! People whose interests are different from your own may enrich your life. They provide fresh topics of conversation and experiences that can expand your own horizons.

5. Join a support group. "I never knew how much support you could get from other women until my divorce," said several women. "Now I wonder how I lived without some of those women."

"I'm a big fan of widows' support groups," said Dot. "You may not fit the first group you go to, so go to several two or three times each until you find one where you fit. It is so helpful to be with others who truly understand what you are going through."

Lori says of her naval wives' group, "Whether you are best buddies or not, you have a strong bond because of your shared experience."

Except for military wives, however, *married* women home alone are prone to live in isolation. Allison is one exception. She says, "Women home alone desperately need to find others in their own situation—people who understand, and who you know don't mind your calling, because they're alone, too. I think I've actually developed a better support system than women whose husbands are home all the time. I feel comfortable calling on women in my own situation, and we give each other a lot of support. Other women provide fellowship, a sounding board about decisions you need to make and little crises, and they and their families provide a place of belonging for your kids."

If you don't have a support group in your area, be the first in your town to start one.

6. Find others who need you. Sometimes the best antidote for our own loneliness is to find someone lonelier. One summer in a new city my sons and I went weekly to conduct an arts and crafts class for children in a homeless shelter. Not only did the children enjoy our coming, but they sure kept us busy.

Next time you are lonely, ask, "Whom do I know who also might be lonely right now? Whom could I make feel better by writing a letter, going by for a cup of tea, or helping out?"

If you don't know anybody personally, call programs that work with the homeless, battered women, illiterates, or the elderly.

One writer declares, "You're only as alone as you want to be. There's a whole world out there.... Is Mother Teresa lonely? I doubt it! Not that I'm recommending everyone to go out and save the world. But saving just a little bit of it may also save you!"[10]

7. If single, seek a spouse. In Scripture, Ruth, Tamar, and Esther all took active parts in finding husbands. Meg Woodson admits that

> Such a role is sometimes shunned by Christian women today [because they] do not want to admit that they could take active steps in bringing that about. The only spiritual option is to pray. Any kind of overt activity on their part would be potentially interfering with God's will, so the argument goes.
>
> But just think about this in regard to some of the day-to-day concerns in our lives. If we are looking for a better job or an apartment ... do we do nothing but pray? Even the most spiritual among us would also be developing a course of action to achieve our goals.... Would it be just as appropriate to develop a course of action in seeking a prospective marriage partner?[11]

How would a single woman go about that? Set a goal, such as "I want to meet so many new men in the next six months" or "I want to be married within the year." Consider your strengths and interests, and pursue them; you are more likely to meet someone you enjoy doing something you both enjoy. Ask friends to introduce you to men they know. Be bold about going to parties alone, but be careful (see page 91). And, as you do your part, pray a lot.

IN CONCLUSION

A woman home alone will inevitably have lonely times. Elisabeth Elliot warns, "In the wilderness of loneliness we are terribly vulnerable. What we want is OUT, and sometimes there appear to be some easy ways to get there.... If we do, we may find a measure of happiness, but not the lasting joy our heavenly Father wants us to have."[12]

On the positive side, loneliness can provide the soil of solitude where we can cultivate seeds of self-reliance and faith. Loneliness can spur us to new interests, deeper friendships, wider service to others.

And on those days when, as August said, we just don't have the gumption to get up and do anything about our loneliness, it's okay to cry.

Since one of the loneliest days is a holiday spent alone, let's look at that now.

Suggested Further Reading

Directory of Support Groups. Widowed Person's Service, AARP, 1909 K Street NW, Washington, DC 20049, 202–728–4370.

Elliot, Elisabeth. *The Path of Loneliness*. Nashville: Thomas Nelson, 1988. Based on her own experience of twice being widowed, plus theological insights into how women can learn godly lessons from loneliness.

Woodson, Meg. *Making It Through the Toughest Days of Grief*. Grand Rapids: Zondervan, 1994. Deals with how to cope with recurring waves of grief on special days and holidays.

CHAPTER FIVE

$\mathcal{H}$ome for the Holidays—Alone

God, it's Thanksgiving. Families are sitting down to roast turkey with dressing. People are laughing with relatives and friends, and I sit alone in my kitchen with a cold ham sandwich, an apple, and a glass of milk. No family. No friends. No turkey. Nothing to look forward to after I finish eating. I tell myself it's just another day—but why do I feel so much more alone?

One of the worst kinds of loneliness is spending a holiday alone. I learned that at twenty-two, when I spent the winter in a Scottish highland village. I boarded in a local guest house where the dining room overlooked heathered hills, and never minded eating alone until one Thursday when I realized, "It's Thanksgiving!" As I contemplated my boiled meat and vegetables and thought about my family eating turkey in Miami, tears ran down my cheeks.

Years later I got behind in my writing, and suggested that Bob take our boys to his mother's for Thanksgiving. I planned to spread notes all over the dining-room table for four days. I worked energetically, delighted with the quiet house, until lunchtime Thursday. Suddenly I felt like a puppy nobody wanted. Why had I urged the others to go without me? I'd thought I was making a wise, mature decision. What I had made was a big mistake.

As Lauren said in her interview, "Holidays alone are terrible!"

Almost any woman may be alone for an occasional holiday or special day. Many women will be alone for most of them. Few enjoy the experience. People who are newly bereaved or divorced find holidays especially painful, but even those accustomed to holidays alone have a hard time celebrating. My friend Grace, single, used to put up a tree and decorate her townhouse every Christmas, but when Hurricane Andrew blew away her decorations she didn't replace them. "Why go to all that bother just for me?" she asked with a shrug. "Nobody saw them, and it was a lot of work."

If you are looking for happy little suggestions of "How to Have a Merry Christmas Alone," this chapter is going to disappoint you. None of the women I interviewed knew how to do that. They and a few other authors, however, have wisdom worth sharing.

YOU THINK IT'S TOUGH BECAUSE IT IS!

A counselor I interviewed for *Women Who Do Too Much* stressed the need for women to "give ourselves permission" to feel and express our feelings. If you're a woman home alone for a special holiday or occasion, give yourself permission to feel sad, lonely, or abandoned. Your feelings are entirely appropriate.

Meg Woodson, writing to new widows in *Making It Through the Toughest Days of Grief*, devotes an entire chapter to "The Special Pain of Special Occasions." Some of what she has to say resonates with any woman who has to spend a special occasion alone:

> The special pain . . . [you feel] on special days is an intensification of the pain you feel every day. . . . Special days are days of tradition, traditions of love, and now these best of traditions have been broken.

To help ease loneliness on special days alone, Woodson suggests:

1. Plan ahead. Build structure—support—into these days. It's being caught off guard that does you in.

2. Take care of yourself on these days. Rest. Treat yourself.
3. Feel the grief triggered by these days. Feel a little of the grief away.
4. Let people hold you on these days.
5. Let God hold your heart in his hands on these days.[1]

MISERY IS ONLY ONE OF YOUR CHOICES

Priscilla describes a birthday after her divorce as a turning point in her life. "My teenage sons, who live with their father, didn't even remember it was my birthday. I went to a flower show alone and felt pretty sad, because I wanted to hear my sons' voices. Finally I realized, 'I am forty-one years old. It's time to start living for myself and not depend on other people to make me happy. It's up to me to make my life what I need it to be. I can't rely on others, not even my family, for my happiness.'"

Alone or not, we women need to know our happiness does not depend on other people. Nor does our misery. Maybe we aren't ecstatic about spending a holiday alone. But must we be miserable?

Just as Joshua gave the people of Israel a choice: "Choose this day whom you will serve" (Joshua 24:15), so life gives us a daily choice: "Choose this day whether you will stay locked in your misery or take steps to get beyond it."

Doreen's divorce came just before her twenty-fifth wedding anniversary. She went on an Alaskan cruise. "Some people take a trip like that for their anniversary. Instead, I took it with some friends. Not as romantic, but hey—we had a good time, and it was far better than staying home moping about what I didn't have."

TRADITIONS HAVE TO START SOMEWHERE

In an article entitled "Family Change: Don't Cancel Holidays!" authors Evan Imber-Black and Janine Roberts suggest, "Find a way to rework the holidays that fits for you."[2] Don't try to have a "holiday as usual" when someone special is absent, they urge. Instead, ask "What about this holiday will I miss the most?" or "What about this holiday do I yearn for most?" Then ask: "What can I provide that will have real meaning for me?"

One family started going camping each Thanksgiving after the parents' divorce. A single woman spends each Christmas on a short Caribbean cruise. Two single women started years ago going to the mountains for Thanksgiving, treating themselves to a bed-and-breakfast inn, lazy mornings, and lots of time to read. They have so much fun that an empty-nest couple now goes along each year.

Is there some place you'd rather be than alone this next holiday? Someone you'd like to see? Something you'd like to do anytime, and can do over a holiday as well as—or better than—another time? If you do something more than once, you may find you have created a tradition!

On the other hand, maybe there are traditions from your past that you want to preserve. You may find that observing the tradition is not as painful as you thought it would be—in fact, it may be less painful than abandoning a tradition and yearning for it. "In . . . times of rapid and dramatic change in the family, rituals can still provide us with a crucial sense of personal identity as well as family connection."[3]

Almost any wife of a traveling man will spend an occasional holiday alone. It helps if the family makes an effort to make up the missed day. Lynn's husband makes frequent trips overseas. "Over the years, he's been out of the country for birthdays and at least one Mother's Day, Father's Day, Memorial Day, and Thanksgiving. When he's away for a birthday, he tries to call, and he often brings us a special gift. We have that to look forward to."

Martha recalls, "He's only missed one of my birthdays, and he sent flowers. I'd never gotten flowers before. I cried from joy."

Military wives probably spend more holidays alone than any other married women. Some families, like Karen's, save all celebrations until Dad finally gets home. Others, like Sue's, celebrate and send pictures to Dad on his ship. In each case, the children of the family know that "This is the way our family celebrates." They are secure in their own family traditions.

REMEMBER, YOU ARE NOT REALLY ALONE

Sue says, "When we're alone for a special holiday, we try to gather other families who are also alone. Fellowship is important."

August, another Coast Guard wife, remembers one Christmas when she was grateful to be on the other end of that kind of concern: "We had just moved to a new base, I was pregnant, and my husband had to be away. Friends we had known at an earlier base called and insisted we come over for Christmas day. 'We know what that's like,' they told me. I still missed my husband, of course, but it wasn't as bad as sitting home by myself with little children."

Frances, a widow, goes to her son's for Christmas and Easter, but sometimes spends Thanksgiving at home. "When I had a problem being alone, I invited others to my house. Everybody brought a little something, and that way nobody was alone and nobody worked too hard. It turned out to be a lot of fun."

A WISE WOMAN KNOWS
I am not the only one in the world who is alone.

YOU MAY BEST KEEP THE OCCASION BY GIVING IT AWAY

Not everyone feels like inviting a crowd of other lonely people home for Christmas. One single woman hosted a very stilted Christmas dinner for other single young adults. "We just sat around all afternoon and felt like losers together." That can be deadly! But there's an alternative that sounds similar, yet is totally different: give your holiday away.

Jesus described a paradox in Luke 9:24: "Whoever would save his life will lose it; and whoever loses his life for my sake will save it."

I discovered how that can work the Christmas I spent in Scotland. After my teary Thanksgiving, I dreaded Christmas whether I spent the day entirely alone or intruded on family celebrations of new friends in my village. Since I was going to be miserable either way, I decided I might as well give Christmas to somebody who otherwise might not have one.

I selected three elderly people with no family and few friends. ("A dour old thing," one was described.) I asked each if I could drop by in the afternoon, and they said I could if I liked. After lunch, I took small gifts and crunched down the snowy hill to make my Christmas calls. I did not go in love and charity. I went wrapped in cheerless, miserable, self-conscious piety. And if I hadn't already said I'd be dropping by, I would have trudged back up the hill to my empty room.

At two of the houses I was received awkwardly. We visited briefly, and I left wondering why I'd bothered to go. The third house was the two-room cottage of Mrs. Harkess, a shy widow. She welcomed me with an invitation to "Come in and sit a wee whiley. We'll just listen to the Queen, then have a cuppa tea."

As the Queen gave her televised Christmas Day speech, my hostess darted from her spartan kitchen to a table by the fire, surreptitiously placing dish after dish on a snowy cloth. By the time the Queen had finished, Mrs. Harkess had spread a feast that must have strained her slender budget. As the afternoon dwindled into early darkness, she regaled me with stories of her childhood on a highland croft, her years of married life, and the long and painful death of her husband. She showed me exquisite embroidered linens she had kept since her marriage three decades before. She brought out musty albums of sepia photographs from the turn of the century. In that one afternoon I learned more about life in Scotland than I had learned in the three months I'd lived there. We also began a friendship that would last the rest of her life.

I'd planned to give my Christmas afternoon to Mrs. Harkess. Instead, Mrs. Harkess gave me one of the best Christmases I've ever had.

Apartments, nursing homes, hospices, homeless feeding programs, and congregational directories are filled with persons who are lonely and isolated. Spending time with them may or may not brighten your own lonely day, but you can certainly brighten theirs if you take the trouble to do so.

My husband reminded me about another segment of lonely people in our society: international students. One Thanksgiving when we were new in a city and not eager to cook a turkey for four, we called a local university and asked if any international students might want to eat with an American family. Two lively Malaysian men came to dinner and became friends.

If you are interested in meeting international students and don't know how to begin, consider Christmas International House, a program that places international students in local congregations over Christmas holidays. While the students sleep and eat most meals at the church, the host congregation almost always needs drivers, meal hosts, and tour guides. Persons who help out with the program get to know students from around the world and usually share an international dinner cooked by the students at the end of their visit. For more information about the program, call the Christmas International House office at 404–938–4291.

Not all experiences of giving away a holiday will be blessed, of course. You may give your holiday to somebody who is cranky, ungrateful, and surly. Still, there is that paradoxical law of the universe: if you want to gain something, you have to let go of it. If you are going to be miserable spending a holiday alone anyway, you might as well give your day to somebody else. Don't expect to get anything back. Then you *may* be pleasantly surprised!

IN CONCLUSION

Consider the next holiday you will need to spend alone. Admit that holidays alone are not much fun. Give yourself permission to feel lonely, sad, even abandoned. Hum a few bars of "It's my party, and I'll cry if I want to."

Give an upcoming holiday some serious thought *now*. If it will bring you grief, how can you structure the day to provide support and people to hold you? If it will be lonely, how can you arrange to spend part of it with some special person? If it will be dull and boring, what could you plan that might make it more fun?

Ask yourself, "What about this holiday will I miss or yearn for the most? What can I substitute that will be meaningful for me instead?" Consider trying something that could become a tradition if it works this time.

Ask, "What traditions from past years meant a lot to me? Which of them would I like to preserve or reinstitute this year?"

Consider whom else you know and enjoy who will be alone on the holiday. Is there something you might do together?

If you can't get excited about any of the other suggestions, consider giving the day away. Somebody out there could be less miserable because you came. And who knows? You might serve in disguise the One who said, "If you show kindness to one of the least of my brothers and sisters, you show kindness to me" (Matthew 25:40).

Suggested Further Reading

Gaither, Gloria, and Shirley Dobson. *Let's Make a Memory: Great Ideas for Building Family Traditions and Togetherness*. Dallas: Word, 1983. While written for families, this book also offers ideas women home alone can use.

Imber-Black, Evan, and Janine Roberts. *Rituals for Our Times*. New York: HarperCollins, 1992. Authors are keenly aware of difficulties for women spending holidays alone.

Woodson, Meg. *Making It Through the Toughest Days of Grief*. Grand Rapids: Zondervan, 1994. Worth mentioning again because in addition to dealing with general tough days, Woodson gives specific good suggestions for particular holidays.

CHAPTER SIX

T Never
Cook Real Food

Lord, guilt is using me like a bench press. We ate out tonight for the third time this week. Are we getting too much junk food? Will it hurt the children? Will they grow up thinking home-cooked food is microwaved leftovers from a doggy bag?

Our family sits down almost every night to a balanced dinner. We talk about the day and get into long discussions about black holes, plots of movies or books, and whether one eats Jello with a fork or a spoon. When one parent goes away, however, we easily slide into a hastily scrambled eggs or take-out pizza routine. Why should one less person make such a difference?

I don't know, but it does.

Most women I interviewed mentioned lighter meals as a natural part of being alone. Some stay overweight from snacks and junk food. Others eat so little you can see their bones. Few cook regular balanced meals unless there's a man at the table. Paula, single, and Priscilla, divorced, each confessed, "I never cook real food." Allison added, "When Scott's gone, I cook far simpler than when he's here." Suzanne admitted, "We don't eat right when he's gone."

There seem to be two options: eat out, or eat much less. Frozen dinners, for instance, were described as "lifesavers" and "comfort food." And while some women felt guilty about going out so often, August—whose Coast Guard husband is often gone two weeks at a time—has a refreshing philosophy about taking her four children to restaurants while he's away: "I have learned which restaurants let kids eat free on which nights, and that's where we go. When he comes home, he's been eating out and so have we. We're all ready for home cooking."

Allison, with three small children, eats out for a different reason. "A friend of mine is a single mom, and we often take the children out and put them at the next table. The meal becomes a social event for everybody."

WAYS TO EAT SMART AT HOME

Eating out all the time gets expensive, and may not offer the balanced nutrition bodies need to stay healthy. What else can a woman home alone do? Here are a few ideas:

1. Planned Overs: Instead of "leftovers," Martha—who has two teenage daughters and a husband who is regularly away three or four days every week—cooks "planned overs": two nights' meals at a time. "We just plan to eat the same thing twice. It's a habit, so nobody even notices."

Lori makes an enormous pot of something, like spaghetti, and eats it for a week. "Luckily I don't get bored with it like some people do."

2. Smart Freezing: Freezing individual pork chops, hamburgers, and chicken sections is an obvious way to cook for one, or even for a mother and children. Ten minutes under the broiler for the meat, ten minutes in the microwave for a baked potato (see page 59), a quick salad, and you have a meal. Some women have made smart freezing an art:

- *Order Chinese food delivered.* Bonnie says, "Since they have a price minimum, I order two full meals—entrees and soup—plus eggrolls, then I repackage the food into individual servings and freeze it. I get five or six meals for fifteen dollars. That's not bad!"

57

- *Cook ahead and freeze single servings.* Judy deliberately cooks extra when her husband is home and freezes portions for her own use when he's away.

  Paula cooks a batch of pancakes and freezes two per plastic zipper bag. "Throw them in a microwave for a minute, and they're ready to eat."

  Sarah Gay freezes a pound of bacon in two-slice packages, so she can take out one serving at a time.

  Paula also orders a medium pizza and freezes individual slices. She has developed a method of thawing it that really makes the pizza taste fresh.

Paula's Frozen Pizza Good as Fresh!

Line cookie sheet with foil.

Place pizza cheese side down on foil.

Place under broiler for 45–60 seconds to warm the crust.

Turn over. Cook 3–5 minutes under broiler to heat the top.

Eat immediately.

3. Backwards Day: When Dad's away, Teale's family sometimes eats breakfast foods for dinner. By giving it a special name, they've made it a special event.

4. Eating Club: Paula suggests arranging with other women home alone (with or without children) to eat together one or two nights a week. Either rotate houses and let each hostess cook, or each bring a couple of dishes.

When I was single and first learning to cook, I deliberately invited guests each Saturday evening and tried out new recipes. I cooked enough for leftovers later in the week. (I also asked my friends to tell somebody where they were eating, so if they got sick on the food, somebody would come looking for me, too!)

RECIPES FOR ONE

Because there are so few cookbooks for one, here are a few easy favorite recipes women volunteered.

Sarah Gay's Super-Quick Stir-Fry

1 chicken breast, boneless, sliced thin	1 carrot, sliced into pennies
1/2 onion	1 squash, sliced
3–5 fresh mushrooms	1/4 head cabbage

1. Cook rice. When it is 10 minutes from finished:
2. In skillet or wok heat 1 T. olive oil until hot.
3. Add 1/4 tsp. salt and dash of powdered garlic.
4. Cook chicken 2–3 minutes, remove.
5. Add 1 T. more oil, heat.
6. Cook vegetables, stirring constantly, until crisp-tender (about 2 minutes).
7. Add chicken, stir until heated. Serve over rice.

One steak sliced thin works equally well.

Frances's Pasta Primavera

1. Cook 12 oz. pasta twists or shells until firm.
2. Toss with small amount of garlic dressing (below) to keep from sticking.
3. Add:

4 oz. green olives, sliced	1 small jar red pimento
1 green pepper, diced	2 cups raw broccoli florets

4. Toss with generous amount of dressing made by blending:

1/2 cup salad oil	3 T. vinegar
1/2 tsp. salt	2 cloves crushed garlic
1/2 cup mayonnaise	

This pasta keeps for days in the refrigerator.

Good as Oven-Baked Microwave Potatoes

1. Stab potato deeply twice with fork and rub with cooking oil.
2. Bake 5–8 minutes on high, until soft. (Test by holding with dish towel and squeezing.)
3. Serve with cheese, bacon, broccoli, and onions for a complete meal.

Personal Pizzas

I must have been the last woman in America to discover these, but in case I am the next-to-last:

1. Spread English muffins or small Boboli with pizza sauce (next to spaghetti sauce on grocer's shelf).
2. Layer each with mozzarella cheese and your choice of toppings.
3. Grill under broiler until cheese melts.

IN CONCLUSION

Cooking for one—or even one woman plus children— is hard to get enthusiastic about. However, with the variety of frozen dinners, increasing numbers of inexpensive "one notch above fast food" restaurants, and salad bars in grocery stores, a woman home alone has little excuse not to eat right these days. Particularly when you consider what can happen if you don't—which is what we consider in the next chapter: women home alone and illness.

Suggested Cookbooks for Women Home Alone

Johnson, Carlean. *Six Ingredients or Less (Over 500 Quick & Easy Recipes)*. Gig Harbor, WA: CJ Books, 1989. The title says it all! Few ingredients to worry about, quick and easy recipes.

Spaude, Pam, and Jan Owan-McMenamin. *One Year of Healthy, Hearty, and Simple One-Dish Meals*. Minneapolis: Chronimed Publishing, Inc., 1993. Low-fat, low-cholesterol delicious and timesaving recipes with suggestions for quick and easy side dishes.

Williams, Chuck, general editor, and Diane Rossen Worthington, author. *Stir-Fry from the Williams-Sonoma Kitchen Library*. New York: Time-Life Custom Publications, 1994. These recipes are so simple and the pictures so gorgeous, you want to make everything at once! This series also has good books on grilling, pasta, and chicken.

CHAPTER SEVEN

When Aspirins Aren't Enough

God, since the porch swing fell on my ankle last night, I can scarcely hobble. Did I crack a bone? Do I need an x-ray? Can I afford an x-ray? Can I afford not to get one if I need it? How will I cope if I have to stay off my feet? Once more, God, I'm utterly dependent on myself and you, and I don't know what to do.

Getting sick or injured while alone is enough to make any woman yearn for her mom. Married women home alone may remember wistfully the "in sickness and health" promise in their marriage ceremony.

Lori had a miscarriage while her husband was at sea. "It's just once again a major thing that happens that he isn't there to share. It doesn't make you angry, because it's useless to get mad, but it's something that makes you sad."

A study by Florida International University revealed that for senior citizens who live alone, their second greatest fear, after crime, is of becoming frail with no one around to help.[1] Women home alone, of all ages, express a similar fear of getting sick or having a serious, immobilizing accident.

When one husband moved to take a new job, he left his wife with a three-year-old and all the packing to do. "I started having chest pains at night after putting my son to bed. Then I saw a news report about a woman who was murdered while at home with a toddler. I don't think the toddler witnessed the killing, but he did stay in the house with the body for a couple of days. I started worrying. What if I had a heart attack and my toddler was left alone in the house with my unconscious or dead body? Even if my husband had tried to call every day—which he couldn't—he wouldn't have thought it unusual to find me out. It could have been days before anybody noticed."

Fortunately, her fears were groundless. Her concern, however, was practical.

Several women I interviewed described frightening medical emergencies they've had to cope with alone. Karen tripped over her younger daughter's cradle and lodged a nail in her ankle bone. Sue developed a reaction to antibiotics that dehydrated her and gave her hallucinations. Judy got a bee sting working in her yard and had an allergic reaction.

Sarah Gay had a kidney stone. "I woke in the middle of one night with the most terrible pain I'd ever had. 'Whom will I call?' I wondered. My neighbors were older women whom I didn't want to bother at that hour. Finally I thought about our choir director, who lives nearby. He drove me to the emergency room."

PREPARE AHEAD FOR MEDICAL EMERGENCIES

Here are twelve ways a woman home alone can prepare for a medical emergency before it happens:

1. *Buy a home health care manual and get familiar with it.* A good health care manual will help you diagnose and treat simple common problems like burns, nosebleeds, insect stings, and head colds. It will also help you know when to go to an emergency room, when a doctor visit is necessary, and when a few days' coddling is all you need. Two good manuals are suggested at the end of this chapter, but you may find one you prefer at your local bookstore. Before buying one, read a few pages and choose one you understand.

62

2. Keep a well-stocked first-aid kit. A good first-aid kit is essential for a woman home alone. You don't want to have to drive across town in the middle of the night (maybe even dragging sleeping children) to get something you've run out of! *Compare your medicine chest with Checklist 2 in the back of this book to be sure you are well-equipped.*

3. Have a doctor BEFORE an emergency.

4. Know the nearest emergency room your doctor uses, and how to get there from your house.

5. Decide before an emergency whom you can call at any hour, both for transportation and for child care, if needed.

6. Post emergency numbers near the phone. "I now keep numbers of people I can call by my phone," Sarah Gay told me. "Deciding whom to call was one of the worst parts of the experience."

7. Keep a telephone handy if you feel dizzy, nauseated, or just plain sick. Minor illnesses can get worse. A cellular or cordless phone is handy to carry around with you.

8. Have a buddy you can call if you get even mildly sick. Doreen says, "If I feel the least bit sick or disoriented, I call my neighbor, a widow. When one of us is sick, the other calls daily to check up. It's a favor we do each other."

Dr. Moira Burke recommends that your buddy should have a duplicate list of your emergency phone numbers to call in case of illness, and a list of any regular medications you take.

9. Give someone you trust a key to your front door, and permission to enter in case of suspected emergency.

10. Take a CPR course with your buddy, so you can help one another.

11. Do all you can to prevent illness. Avoid people with flu or colds, take flu shots, keep tetanus shots up-to-date, have annual checkups and Pap smears. What is merely common sense for other women is far more important for a woman who has to battle illness alone.

12. Avoid alcohol abuse. While I was writing this book, I heard a radio statistic that one-third of the twelve thousand alcoholics in this country are women. Dr. Burke points out that this can be a serious health issue for women home alone. "Alcohol abuse can come from a combination of loneliness and a lot of time on your hands," she says. "If you feel you find solace in one or two drinks alone and it becomes a habit, you need to seek help."

TREATING BURNS

Burns are one of the most common household emergencies. You'll note that one item on Checklist 2 is an aloe plant for your kitchen. Nothing works quicker than aloe in healing a simple burn. To use, cut a large aloe leaf, slit it, and rub the burned area with the slimy inside of the leaf. Within seconds burning stops, and the burn begins to heal.

It is important to buy an aloe with white, not yellow, sap. Ask permission to break off one leaf and split it to see the color of the interior. Yellow sap can be irritating to skin.

For third-degree burns, in which the skin is burned so deeply that the patient may not even feel pain, DO NOT APPLY ANYTHING! Wrap in a clean sheet and rush to the emergency room. A life could be at stake.

EATING WHEN YOU'D JUST RATHER DIE

When I was sick as a child, my mother used to bring tempting little trays, with doilies and sometimes a flower, right to my bedside. Do you suppose my frequent illnesses as a child had anything to do with those wonderful little trays?

A woman home alone, alas, seldom has anybody to bring her tempting trays. Most of us curl up beneath the blankets and try to pretend we aren't really hungry. However, that voice you hear is not your mother, it's common sense: "You need to eat to build up your strength." Doctors advise, when sick:

- Drink lots of water, fruit juices, broths, and thin soups.
- Eat small, frequent meals.
- Fix your favorite foods first, to stimulate your appetite.

- Take advantage of times when you feel slightly better (in the morning, for instance) to fix your largest meal of the day.
- Steer clear of fats, which are hard on the digestive system.
- Avoid dairy products except, perhaps, yogurt.

A Simple, Nutritious Meal

Throw canned or fresh fruit (bananas and frozen strawberries are particularly delicious), yogurt, and wheat germ into a blender with 3-4 ice cubes and half a cup of orange juice. Yields a quick, frosty, nutritious drink that's easy to swallow and digest.

Food Is Medicine

A growing body of scientific evidence suggests that proper nutrition, stress reduction, and support from friends and family are important in helping our bodies fight illness.

"Food," says Dr. Susan Finn, president of the American Dietetic Association, "should be treated just like a medicine. . . . When you're sick, your glands are pumping out hormones in response to the physical stress of infection and illness, and your immune system's frantically trying to put out fires. That speeds up your metabolism—meaning that you're drawing on your body's reserves, including vitamins and minerals. If your nutrient intake is poor, your recovery can stall, and you set yourself up for infection and numerous other complications."[2]

Who needs complications?

Therefore, a woman home alone needs a "First-Aid Pantry," certain foods she keeps in stock that she can easily fix and eat if she gets sick. *Check your pantry against Checklist 3.*

And if friends call and ask, "What can I do?" don't hesitate to point out that a spare casserole, salad, or soup would be most welcome!

LEARNING FROM WOMEN WITH CHRONIC ILLNESS

Perhaps the bravest of all women home alone are those who deal daily with a chronic illness.

Lynn said, "Illness has greatly complicated our lives. I was diagnosed with chronic fatigue syndrome seven years ago, and in the beginning I was eighty percent debilitated. Then our daughter was also diagnosed with CFS. When we realized that this was a long-term condition, my husband and I had to ask, 'What does this mean? Will Bas have to leave his job and not travel?' He was willing to do whatever was needed, but we felt he was called to the job, and we both wanted him to do it.

"At that point, his office staff and our church stepped in. They took turns, two weeks each, and they took care of me and our daughter while he was gone. They did meals, errands, whatever we needed. One incredible friend did my listening and heard my crying. My husband was able to maintain his travel schedule, and the stress was not destructive."

Jill, whose husband is a publishing executive, had a similar experience. "Nine years ago I got lupus. I have begun to get better at asking people for wisdom, and when I need something done, I'm better at calling on neighbors to ask, 'Whom should I call?' Also, if I get overcommitted and the lupus flares, it's hard for me to back out of a commitment, but I'm beginning to accept that I have to. Three times in nine years I've had major flare-ups of a couple of months each. I've had to learn to live with that."

Without minimizing at all the tremendous amounts of courage and determination it takes for those women to support their husbands in their traveling work, let us look at what they have discovered that other women home alone need to know:

Call on other people when you need them. Some studies have linked low levels of social support with a higher incidence of heart disease, stomach ulcers, headaches—even early death after a heart attack.[3] You are *not* a wimp if you call on someone to help when you are sick. You are being smart. Next time, they may have to call on you!

If you overcommit, back out. The rest of the world may not appreciate the amount of energy it takes for a woman home alone to maintain a house, a job and/or children, and outside commitments. Only you know what your maximum time is for volunteer commitments. Sometimes it is important for physical, spiritual, or mental health to back away.

IN CONCLUSION

Being home alone is tough enough, without having to be sick alone, too. Take steps while you are well to make sick days easier on yourself. Find a doctor. Decide whom to call in emergencies. Get a health manual. Get a "health buddy." Stock a first-aid kit and a first-aid pantry. And take steps to stay healthy!

Good Medical References to Have on Hand

Lenox-Hill Medical School. *The Lenox-Hill Hospital Book of Symptoms and Solutions.* New York: Random House, 1994. An excellent guide to help you know what various symptoms mean and what to do about them.

Simons, Anne, M.D., Bobbie Hasselring, and Michael Castleman. *Before You Call the Doctor.* New York: Fawcett Columbine, 1992. Practical steps for home treatment before seeing a doctor; also describes symptoms that need medical evaluation and treatment.

Suggested Further Reading

Vanderzalm, Lynn. *Finding Strength in Weakness: Help and Hope for Families Battling Chronic Fatigue Syndrome.* Grand Rapids: Zondervan, 1995. Written by a woman who not only has chronic fatigue syndrome herself, but has a daughter with the same condition—and a husband whose work requires international travel. Practical and full of hope.

CHAPTER EIGHT

Things That Go Bump in the Night

From ghoulies and ghaisties,
Long-legged beasties,
And things that go bump in the night,
Good Lord deliver us.
　　　　　Old Scottish Prayer

As I said earlier, it was a single woman saying she is some-times still nervous at night that first drew my attention to women home alone. Nighttime fears or nervousness are, for some women, a very hard part of living alone. "I turn on the television when my husband is away," Allison cheerfully admits. "It makes me think there's somebody in the house."

Author Barbara Holland wryly describes these fears: it is as if "the absence of other people in the room has created a vacuum, into which murderers will surely be sucked."[1] We may chuckle at that in the daylight, but for many women home alone, fear is no laughing matter after dark. How can we deal with nighttime fears?

SEEK A BALANCE BETWEEN FEAR AND FOOLISHNESS

It is no wonder many women home alone are afraid. Newspaper and television reporters work hard to convince us there's a rapist behind every bush, a carjacker in every parking lot, a murderer creeping toward our beds every night. Our statistic-loving nation counts crimes with relish: "Chillingly, in this country, a private home is robbed every ten seconds. In one of every twelve robberies, victims suffer serious injury. In close to one percent of those brutal crimes, the victim is also raped."[2]

A survey by the Center for Media and Public Affairs showed that the three major TV networks aired more than twice as many crime stories in 1993 as in 1992, even though the nation's crime rate remained virtually unchanged. As a result, the public's fear of crime reached record highs.[3]

While some women are terrified by a steady diet of crime statistics and eleven o'clock television crime reports (euphemistically labeled "The Evening News"), other women shrug and say, "Violent crime happens to other people. It won't happen to me." They dismiss advice on how to protect themselves as fear mongering and, like the foolish virgins in Jesus' parable, fail to prepare.

A wise woman home alone maintains a sane balance between knowing on the one hand that violence is very real, and knowing on the other hand that she is not in constant danger. She takes some practical steps, such as those described in the following chapters, to secure herself and those she loves. She takes equally practical steps to insure her peace of mind.

WORK ON PEACE OF MIND

Several years ago when we lived in westside Chicago, my purse was snatched twice within six months. After the second time, I stopped carrying purses. I walked uneasily down sidewalks. Two weeks later, when I went into our front yard to photograph my three-year-old, I saw a man start across the street toward us. I froze! I knew without a shadow of a doubt that he was coming to take my camera. And while every impulse shouted "Run!" I could not move.

My legs trembled. My teeth chattered. I waited, paralyzed and terrified, to be victimized again.

Actually, the man had recognized me from a church picnic the previous summer. He was merely coming over to say hello.

I read later that fear lasts ninety days after a panic situation. I believe it. A woman home alone who has been the victim of a violent crime needs to give herself time to get over it. Getting over it, however, is essential. Nothing is as paralyzing as fear, and fear distorts the rest of the world.

Both panic and courage reinforce themselves. To decrease panic and build courage, therefore, try this:

1. *Exercise common sense—and I do mean exercise.* Give it a good workout! Common sense reminds us that being alone doesn't automatically make us more vulnerable than other people. Houses with men in them also have fires, accidents, and burglaries. "Solitude," Holland reminds us, "is only marginally more dangerous than life with people. It just feels that way."[4]

Common sense also looks at crime statistics for comfort as well as caution. In the statistic previously quoted, one robbery every ten seconds equals 8,640 a day in the entire country. Of those, only one in twelve, or 720, will result in serious injury; eleven out of twelve, or 7,920, will not. Only sixty-nine robberies on a given day in the entire country will involve a rape. While we deplore the fact that sixty-nine women may be raped during burglaries in our country today, and exercise caution in our homes, our common sense points out the slim odds that we will be one of the victims.

Common sense may also suggest ways to arrange our lives to cut down on the likelihood we'll become victims of violent crimes. When June and her husband moved to a new city and knew he'd be away many nights, they made choices that could increase her security and peace of mind while he was away. June explains, "Instead of buying a house, we bought a condo with twenty-four-hour security, convenient grocery stores, and nearby bus lines. My daughter can get to school and come home from cheerleading by bus, and there's a security guard to protect her until I get home. I don't drive, so I take a bus to work and a cab at night. That way, I never have to worry about a car breaking down."

Sometimes common sense even helps us to freely admit our own foolishness, laugh indulgently at ourselves, and permit us a bit of eccentricity. After our first baby was born, I found I wasn't as afraid of the dark if I kept him with me. What protection did I expect a five-week-old to provide? I don't know, but he always slept with me when his daddy was gone. I felt much braver.

Similarly, when our younger son was five, he assured me if I would buy him a stuffed lion dressed like David about to fight Goliath, "It will make me brave. I promise!" He needed bravery at that point, but the lion cost more than I wanted to pay for a stuffed animal. When he continued to insist, however, that "David Lion" would make him brave, I bought it—even knowing a toy lion could not make a small boy brave. Do you know what? It did.

Like Allison, my aunt and uncle, both widowed, sleep with a radio on at night to pretend there's somebody in their houses.

If something makes you feel brave, do it.

2. Fill your mind with positives, not negatives. In the musical *The King and I*, Anna sings about whistling a happy tune when she feels afraid. Some of us can't whistle, but we can drag our minds from darkness into light. By force, if necessary. Singing happy songs, listening to happy music, reading happy books—all these can counteract fear. Remember what the Apostle Paul urges in Philippians 4:8? "Whatever is true, whatever is noble, whatever is right, whatever is pure, whatever is lovely, whatever is admirable—if anything is excellent or praiseworthy—think about such things."

That's especially good advice for women home alone.

We choose what goes into our minds. The media makes its living out of getting people excited, and few things are more exciting than fear. Therefore, the media—even, regrettably, often the Christian media—rouses fear to keep us tuned in and their advertisers happy. Peace, joy, and beauty get far less coverage, because they are so much less stimulating.

Peace, joy, and beauty are, however, equally real. We don't have to let the media entertain us with stories about how awful and frightening the world is. If that kind of program or news comes on, we can switch channels or turn it off. After all, God has not retired. Evil is not in the driver's seat.

Likewise, we need to realize that fear is contagious. It may be wise to share with other people the fact that we are afraid, but being in a group of women trying to outdo one another with scary stories is the scariest thing I know. When we are in a group that starts that kind of conversation, we can either excuse ourselves or say gently, "Sorry, folks, but this kind of talk just makes me more scared. Can we change the subject?" You may be doing somebody else a favor, too.

As a writer of mystery novels, I think mysteries are great bedtime reading, but not when I'm alone. Particularly not those that frighten me. When alone, I keep lighthearted amiable books beside my bed: gardening books, devotional books, joke books, P.G. Wodehouse novels, and novels that inspire.

Martha, whose husband is away three or four nights a week, says, "Because fear of terror by night can be overwhelming, I am careful what I read or watch on television. I don't read or watch anything that has to do with stalking, rape, even religious documentaries on demons. I don't let the children watch or read them, either. They are not helpful to us."

SET UP A SECURITY SUPPORT NETWORK

People who live with others have somebody who cares when they get home and sounds an alarm if they don't show up. They also have somebody around when they're worried or nervous. A woman home alone needs to create that kind of caring network for herself, both for her own peace of mind and to help watch her home.

Allison has a divorced friend with whom she checks in each night. "We call each other and say, 'I'm locking my doors now.'"

Bonnie, who lives alone and is in a wheelchair, subscribes to a service that gives her a beeper to wear around her neck. She knows that in case of an intruder or fire, help is one button push away.

Some women arrange to let someone know when they arrive home after night events. Lori, a navy wife whose husband is gone for months at a time, says, "I am very conscious of letting people know where I am. Because I am by myself so much, I could be hurt or dead for days and nobody would know. When I'm out at night, my brother makes me call him when I get home. If I'm going to take off, I let him know where I'm going and when I leave. That way if something happened, he'd have a time frame."

"People need to know where you are," Priscilla agrees, "but that means you have to check in with them, too. One night I'd told my sons I'd call them when I got home from work. Instead, I stopped by a friend's, and she invited me to stay for dinner. My son got worried about ten-thirty and called my preacher. He and his wife went over to my place, found my house dark and my car gone. They called everybody they knew to call, and when nobody knew where I was, they called the police. I arrived home to find blue lights flashing. I was so embarrassed. But I was glad somebody cared that much about where I was."

In addition to someone to watch over her, a woman home alone also needs somebody to watch her home. My husband blames the demise of the front porch for much of today's increased crime. "When people sat on their front porches, they knew what was going on in a community. Now we stay inside and watch television while our neighbor is robbed."

Some communities have formal Crime Watch programs. If yours does not, get to know at least one neighbor and mutually agree to watch one another's homes. Doreen, divorced with grown sons, recalls, "I came home late one night, and my neighbor called. 'You had a prowler.' It turned out to have been one of my son's friends coming to stay for the night, but it was great to have that support system at work."

PRAY WITHOUT CEASING

Martha says, "At night as we go to bed, I pray a hedge of protection around our home, that nothing evil will come in through the door, window, or telephone. Then we go to bed and sleep."

Paula adds, "Sometimes in the night when I wake up and don't know why, I lie awake and listen. But if I hear nothing, I turn it over to God, saying, 'You are more capable of protecting me than I am.'"

I've been cursed all my life with an irrational fear of the dark. During a power outage I'd rather be on a sidewalk than inside a dark house. Over the years, therefore, I've marked "bravery" passages in my Bible. If I wake hearing something bump in the night, I turn on the light and read passages like Psalm 23, "Even though I walk through the valley of the shadow of death, I will fear no evil," and Psalm 134, "Come, bless the LORD, all you servants of the LORD, who stand by night in the house of the LORD!" (RSV) Servants of God standing by night in the house of the Lord. Isn't that a wonderful image?

Some nights I fall asleep quoting a line from George MacDonald's *Diary of an Old Soul*: "The dark still is God."[5]

IN CONCLUSION

Personal security begins with peace of mind. Common sense, wisdom, wholesome thoughts instead of fear, support from others, and prayer can help balance the craziness of the world we often seem to live in.

On the other hand, there is craziness out there. Violence happens. Even though she sleeps in peace, a wise woman home alone will take steps to minimize the likelihood that violence will happen to her. Part Two suggests some of those steps.

Suggested Further Reading

Psalm 91

PART TWO

A Sane Look
at Security

INTRODUCTION

Nobody wants to live in constant fear, but nobody wants to be foolish about security, either. Sane security for a woman home alone involves

- developing commonsense habits and
- taking wise precautions to insure both safety and peace of mind.

The following chapters contain practical suggestions from police officers, several authors, and many women home alone for steps any woman can take to

- make a home more secure,
- stay safe in the car,
- stay safe in public places, and
- stay safe around other people.

Chapter 13 tells what to do if you are the victim of a crime.

Because a woman home alone needs to be more self-reliant than other women, these precautions are very important. However, the ones you need to take will vary from woman to woman and community to community. Mark items you want to implement, then *do* them!

Most of us yearn for a world where violence is ended. Until that day comes:

- Develop safe habits.
- Plan ahead for trouble.
- Stay alert.

CHAPTER NINE

*M*aking Your Home More Secure

Our homes and automobiles are generally safe. We are in greatest danger when we are careless, or permit someone else to enter uninvited. Here are suggestions for making any home more secure.

FIREPROOF YOUR HOME

We start here because fire is the leading cause of accidental death in the United States. Six ways to prevent or cope with fire:

1. Respect electricity. Do not: overload sockets, place extension cords under a rug, or plug extension cords together. Any of those can overload a circuit and cause fires. Electrical appliances need air around them to vent the heat they produce. Do not cover them with newspapers, blankets, or clutter.

2. Respect household chemicals. Do not store paint removers, glue, gasoline, or paint near open flames, a gas furnace, or a water heater.

3. Never place cloth or clothing near a heater or open flame.

4. Keep fire extinguishers and smoke detectors in your home.

5. Establish a "fire alarm plan." Plan how to get out of each room. If you have an upstairs, you may want to invest in a simple fire ladder, available at hardware stores. If you have children, agree on a family meeting place in case of fire and impress on everyone the importance of going straight there and waiting for the others. *In case of fire, get out of the house before you call for help.*

TEN COMMONSENSE HABITS

1. Lock accessible doors and windows when you are at home. Many home burglaries occur on a warm day when doors and windows are wide open or someone is working in the backyard with the front door unlocked or garage door open. Unlocked sheds can also provide a hiding place for an unwanted visitor.

A WISE WOMAN KNOWS
I lock doors when I go out
to protect my possessions.
I lock doors when I am at home
to protect my life.

2. Don't work alone at home in clothes—or lack thereof—that would entice a Peeping Tom.

3. Don't open your door to a stranger. Letting a stranger in to use the phone is the most common factor in women attacked at home. If someone needs a call made, leave them outside and make it for them.

4. Lock the door and the garage door when you'll just be out briefly. Paula reports, "In one apartment I lived in, my neighbor left her door unlocked while she ran over to the mailboxes. Her upstairs neighbor saw her leave, slipped down, and unlocked her bedroom window. Then he came back during the night and raped her."

5. Put away garden tools after use. One burglar used a ladder left outside to reach a second-story window, then used the trowel left beside the ladder to break the glass.

6. Don't tell a stranger that you are alone. Ask a man to tape your answering machine message. Don't mention that you live alone when arranging for deliveries or repairs, and if unfamiliar workmen must come inside, say something like "We're going to be so glad to get the plumbing fixed," or display a hard hat prominently on your entry-hall table. You can even ask a neighbor to drop in for a cup of tea while they work, if you are uneasy.

7. **When you are away in the evening, leave lights on and a radio or television on in a room with closed blinds.**

8. **Don't leave valuables or purses where they can be seen through windows.**

9. **Take extra care when you go out of town.** Cancel the newspaper. Put a note in your mailbox asking the post office to hold your mail until the day after you plan to return. Have your lawn mowed or your snow shoveled. Doreen said, "When I go away, I ask my neighbor to park his extra car in my drive, and I tell him, 'I'll be out of town. If you see a truck in the drive, please watch. If they are delivering something, that's fine. If they are taking something away, call the police!'"

10. **Photograph or engrave a code number on valuables for easy identification if stolen.** Many police stations have engraving pens you can borrow.

INTRUDER-PROOF YOUR HOME

1. **Choose a secure apartment or house.** Select apartments where entryways, parking lots, and laundry facilities are well lit and reasonably secure, and houses with neighbors in hailing distance. If you have an elevator, avoid riding with men you don't know—even if you have to pretend to go back for something you've forgotten. Get to know your neighbors, and spearhead a local apartment or neighborhood watch so neighbors can look out for each other.

2. **Have sturdy doors and locks.** External doors should be solid wood or metal, with dead bolts extending at least an inch into the wood and anti-shim plates on the door frame that cannot be pried out. Paula has an extra dead bolt that doesn't show from the outside. In high-risk areas, consider getting a Door Club, or wedge a chair tightly under the doorknob of exterior doors.

Rekey locks when you move in, to prevent former tenants (or their unsavory friends with keys) from coming back.

Place a rod, pole, or cutoff broomstick into the track of sliding doors to prevent their being popped out of their frames.

"Anybody could break the glass and pick up the sticks," you argue. Sure, but you'd hear them break the glass.

3. Leave a key with a trusted neighbor for emergency use.

4. Burglar-proof your windows. Sarah Gay reports, "One morning I found a screen off my kitchen window and my back gate open. The police said a man in my neighborhood had broken into another house and raped someone that very night. He couldn't raise my window because it was painted shut. After that, I put burglar bars on windows I want to open and left the others painted shut."

If you don't want burglar bars or painted windows, drill a hole in the outer edge of the sash where the upper and lower sashes overlap when the window is closed. Insert a large nail in the hole to join the two sashes together. You can easily remove it when you want to open the window, but when in place it makes it impossible to raise the window.

If you do get burglar bars, be sure they can be opened from inside in case of fire.

5. Give your house a protected look. Trim bushes and get rid of clutter inside an open garage that could provide a hiding place for an unwanted intruder.

6. Put in an alarm system—or buy a decal saying you have one. Radio Shack, for one, sells the decals. If someone calls offering to come out and show you a security system, do not say, "I don't have a system" or "I don't want a system," say, "We are satisfied with the system we have." If you want to buy a system, call the company yourself so you know who is really coming.

7. Buy a barking dog—or make a tape of a friend's dog barking. Play the tape at irregular intervals. Buy a "Beware of the Dog" sign even if you don't have a dog. (I prefer one that reads, "Caution: Boa May Be Loose.")

8. Install security lighting. Doreen points out, "Leaving a house with the same lights on again and again is a dead giveaway that you are gone, if somebody's watching. I installed motion sensor lights at my garage and at my front porch, and bought timers for two lights that come on every night, whether I'm here or not. They come on at different times, too. One in the living room comes on even before I get home and one in the front bedroom comes on at nine and goes off after I usually go to bed. Because they come on every night, nobody can tell when I'm out."

For less than ten dollars a month, the power company will install a security light in your yard, if you have aboveground power poles. We had one of these in a city backyard, and found it made us and our neighbors feel more secure.

Teale, who lives on a large lot, has four switches beside her bed that turn on spotlights at each corner of her house. "If I hear the dog barking, I flip on the lights."

In high-crime areas, ask your police departments to send an officer out to suggest ways to further burglar-proof your home.

AVOID TELEPHONE INTRUSION

The telephone permits strangers free access to our homes. It can cause special problems for a woman home alone. Three particularly disturbing types of calls:

The Call Seeking Information

If a stranger calls and wants to know either your number or name, disconnect gently but firmly.

WRONG:

Caller: "What number is this?"

Woman Home Alone (WHA): "555–7089."

Caller: "Is George there?"

WHA: "There's no George here. I live alone."

If the caller is looking for a victim to harass with obscene calls, he's found one.

RIGHT:

Caller: "What number is this?"

WHA: "What number did you want?"

Caller: "555–7089."

WHA: "Whom did you want?"

Caller: "George."

WHA: "Sorry, you've got the wrong information. We don't have a George in our family. Good-bye." Hangs up.

That caller doesn't know if he's reached a woman home alone or a women with a husband and seven stalwart sons.

Unwanted Sales Calls

While the phone company promises you can put your name on a list of persons not to receive calls, that won't stop most solicitors. Each woman must decide how to handle those calls firmly and quickly. One that works is to say crisply, "We never buy anything over the phone" and hang up before they start their spiel.

"Sales" calls may be soliciting information for theft or scams. Never answer questions over the telephone about your family, income level, security system, credit cards, type of work, or products you use. That information can be translated into when your house is empty and what's likely to be found there.

Scam operators may also use telephone announcements like "You have just won . . ." or "We are going to be doing special demonstrations in your neighborhood" to suck you into a dishonest scheme. If you have genuinely won something, you will be notified by mail.

Obscene Calls

Obscene calls leave most of us feeling degraded and sick. To avoid or minimize those calls:

- List your initials, not your name, in the phone book.
- As soon as you realize it is an obscene call, hang up. If the person was calling numbers at random, you've lost him.
- Keep a whistle beside your phone. Blow it hard into an obscene caller's ear.
- If calls persist, ask your phone company about call tracing and/or caller ID services. Call tracing provides a legal record of any number, which can be used for prosecution. Caller ID lists numbers that call you from your service area. Each costs a small fee, but may help you get rid of the calls.
- "Pray aloud for the person over the phone," says Judy. "That's the quickest deterrent of all."

IN CONCLUSION

Staying safe at home is a matter of developing safe habits and of making certain reasonable precautions are taken to secure doors and windows. It is also a matter of taking charge of the telephone so that you receive only callers you choose.

Suggested Further Reading

Crime-Proof: Protecting Yourself, Your Family, and Your Property. Kansas City: Andrews and Mc Meel, 1994. A comprehensive guide to personal security written by the staff of Knight Ridder Publications.

Safety Tips for Women Alone. Alabama Department of Public Safety, Public Information/Education Dept., P.O. Box 1511, Montgomery, AL 36102–1511.

Spring, Beth. *Staying Safe.* Grand Rapids: Zondervan, 1994. Prison Fellowship's guide to crime prevention with a foreword by Charles W. Colson.

CHAPTER TEN

Staying Safe in Your Car

Staying safe in a car, like staying safe in a home, involves developing commonsense habits and taking reasonable security precautions. It also involves deciding what you would do in case of emergency before one happens to you.

DEVELOP COMMONSENSE HABITS

1. Lock doors when driving. Always! Locking the doors should be as automatic as fastening your seat belt. Who wants a surprise rider when you've stopped for a light or traffic?

2. Keep car doors locked in the driveway. Nothing feels quite as foolish as going outside and discovering your unlocked car has driven away. And don't ask how I know. . . .

3. Unlock only one door at a time. It's a temptation to unlock all doors when you unlock one to put packages in. Don't! One night my father helped my mother into the passenger seat, pushed the automatic button to unlock the driver's door, and went around the car. Before he reached the driver's seat, a drunk had opened the back door and climbed in behind Mother. Dad, a pastor with experience handling drunks, could talk the man into getting out. Someone else might not be so adept.

4. Look in the backseat before you get into your car.

5. Keep your purse between your left side and the door when driving, or at your feet when riding as a passenger. Unless you have seen someone smash a car window and grab a purse from a front seat, you would not believe how quickly it can happen.

6. Keep your car well maintained, and your gas tank half full. Especially if you must drive at night. Get used to checking your oil and tires and listening for noises that may indicate engine trouble. Fix them sooner rather than later. Women alone don't need breakdowns in isolated places or empty gas tanks where they can't choose the service station.

A WISE WOMAN KNOWS
A half-empty gas tank is as easy to fill as an empty one.

TAKE SENSIBLE PRECAUTIONS

1. Plan routes through familiar territory and well-lit streets. Most of us have favorite shortcuts and lovely drives. However, busy streets are generally safer than deserted roads, and well-lit streets safer than dark ones at night. Martha said, "We live fifteen miles from church, and I drive alone to choir practice and evening services. There's a shortcut, but my husband asks me to stay on main streets with lights and people."

2. Keep a spare car key in a pocket or hidden on the car in case your purse is stolen.

3. Carry in your wallet a card listing the vehicle ID number, license number, insurance company, and make and model of your car in case your car gets stolen.

4. Consider getting a cellular phone. Being able to call for help in an emergency can relieve anxiety. It could even save your life!

5. Locate the police station and fire station nearest your home. If you think you are being followed, you will know where to drive instead of going home.

6. In high-crime neighborhoods, try not to stop hemmed in by traffic. Leave space ahead of you for maneuvering into another lane.

7. Stay alert at all times when driving. Don't let yourself get lulled by music or news.

8. Keep a map of your area in your car at all times.

9. Consider installing a security device in your car. These come in a variety of forms: alarms, tracking systems that help the police locate a stolen car, steering wheel locks, window ID systems that etch the vehicle ID into each window, and collars for steering columns. One of the simplest and apparently most effective is "The Club," which prevents the wheel from being turned. Any of the devices listed can deter theft and lower your insurance rates.

PLAN AHEAD FOR EMERGENCIES

A woman who has already considered what she would do in an emergency is more likely to stay calm and respond effectively. Here are some procedures you can decide on ahead:

1. If followed, go to a police station, fire station, busy gas station, or mall. Being followed is a terrifying feeling. Your first impulse may be to hurry home. Don't! There, you are alone and vulnerable. Instead, go to a busy service station, mall parking lot, all-night grocery store, or nearest police station. (You did locate it ahead of time, didn't you?) If you see a police cruiser en route, flash your lights and blow your horn.

2. If someone tries to get into your car, blow the horn and don't stop. Duck down on the seat if the intruder is armed, but drive away as fast as you can.

3. If you get hit from the rear and suspect carjackers, don't stop! They expect you to get out to inspect your damage. Instead, motion for them to follow you and drive to the nearest police station.

4. When driving alone at night and stopped by a red light, drive through with caution if someone approaches your car. Yes, you are breaking the law. On the other hand, a woman was raped in suburban Atlanta several years ago. She had stopped at 2:00 A.M. for a school crossing light the rapist had activated before hiding in nearby bushes. Late at night at an empty intersection, if you see someone coming toward you, risk a fine and run the light.

5. *If you do develop car trouble:* raise the hood, tie something light colored to the door handle nearest the road, get inside, lock your doors, wait, and pray for the right person to stop. When help comes, ask them to send someone from a service station or a police officer to you.

CHAPTER ELEVEN

Staying Safe in Public Places

A woman who lives alone is in no more danger on the street than any other woman, but these days all women have to avoid both careless behavior and paranoia. All strangers are not out to get us—but one or two might be! We do well to take sensible precautions when carrying money, walking or jogging alone, shopping, and getting money from automatic teller machines.

Some women become victims because they've been ruthlessly stalked, but most woman victims have simply failed to observe commonsense methods of reducing their risk. Here are tips for being street-smart.

DEVELOP COMMON SENSE ABOUT MONEY

1. Carry your purse close to your body.

2. When you walk alone and must carry a wallet, carry your money and credit cards in two different places. Always carry enough money in a pocket to get home.

3. Use ATM machines in protected or very visible locations. If you must use an unprotected one, note who else is in the vicinity.

If driving, *never* leave your keys and purse in your car while you use the machine. At night, try to get someone to go with you. Preferably someone very big and mean looking.

USE COMMON SENSE WHEN SHOPPING

1. When leaving a store, stay alert to your surroundings. If you think someone is following you, return to the store and ask one of the employees to walk you to your car.

2. Don't load yourself with packages that obstruct your vision and make it hard to react in case of emergency.

3. When approaching your car, have keys in your pocket or closed fist. You want to be able to unlock your car, get in quickly (after checking the rear seat), and lock the doors. You do *not* want to fumble around for your keys, or dangle them enticingly on a finger. If unlocking a door to unload packages, do not automatically unlock all other doors as well. I told in Chapter 10 how my parents got a surprise one night. You don't want an unwelcome traveler using an unlocked door to join you on your trip home.

4. Avoid shopping at night. If you have to shop at night, shop with a friend if possible, and park under lights and close to the store. Your safety is worth driving around a while waiting for a space. Drive farther if you can get a parking lot with a security guard. Don't window-shop at night, except in malls with security personnel and lots of people.

USE COMMON SENSE WHILE WALKING OR JOGGING

1. Walk or jog with someone else if possible.

2. If you choose to or must walk alone, inform someone of your routine and route. Vary it from time to time.

3. Maintain a steady pace and look calm and confident. Make it clear you know what you are doing and where you are going. Psychologist Elizabeth Davis writes, "Appearing timid or uncertain will always make a woman a more likely target for a sexual attack."[1] I would add, call on angels to protect you, and walk like a person with a bodyguard!

4. Stay alert to who is near you. Look at the people you pass so they know you see them. Headsets and music can make you less alert to your surroundings.

5. Stick to well-lit streets with people, houses, and stores.

6. Don't accept a ride from someone you don't know.

7. If there are bushes that could hide a predator, cross the street.

8. Leave valuable jewelry at home. Turn rings so the stones are toward your palm.

USE COMMON SENSE IN ELEVATORS AND STAIRWELLS

1. If you feel nervous about someone with whom you might have to share an elevator, wait for the next one.

2. Avoid stairwells if you feel uneasy about them. Two teachers left school one afternoon and started to take the stairs. Both felt uneasy. One took an elevator instead. The other laughed at herself, used the stairs, and was attacked on her way down.[2]

A WISE WOMAN KNOWS
Instinct is a gift of God.
If you feel uneasy, retreat.

CHAPTER TWELVE

*S*taying Safe
Around Other People

The world today has more than twice the people it had in 1930. That's a lot more strangers than there used to be. And while most of us want to remain open to the biblical instruction "Do not forget to entertain strangers, for by so doing some people have entertained angels without knowing it" (Hebrews 13:2), women home alone nevertheless need to exercise healthy caution to avoid situations we cannot or don't want to have to handle.

COMMON SENSE ABOUT STRANGERS

1. Be cautious about accepting a ride from someone you don't know. Just because that person has attended the same meeting or even the same church service doesn't mean he or she was there for the same purpose you were.

2. If you leave with someone you do not know, tell someone else whom you are leaving with. Point him or her out, and let the driver know you've told someone: "I told Mary Smith you were driving me home so she needn't bother."

COMMON SENSE ABOUT DATES[1]

Some men beat up on women, and more than half of all rapes are committed by someone the victim knows. When getting to know a new man, stay alert and use your common sense.

Danger Signs that You may be Dating "Mr. Wrong"

He wants to be "the boss," making all the decisions and brushing away your ideas.

He betrays hostile or negative feelings about other women, but says he doesn't feel that way about you. He treats you like a lady, but doesn't show the same respect for others.

He tries to move the relationship ahead too quickly.

He doesn't respect your privacy or space, and wants details about your previous romances.

Wise Behavior on Dates with Strangers and New Men

Never leave a party alone with a man you have just met. Hollywood makes that look romantic; reality makes it dangerous.

Before a first date alone, check him out with people who know him. You aren't prying, you are interviewing.

On first dates, go to a public place. Double-date if you can.

Make sure you have money to get home if you need to.

Don't get drunk or high with a man you don't know—or with one you do.

If You Think You Are in Danger:

Be assertive. First be firm. If that doesn't work, be rude—he is.

Don't plead. Instead, look him squarely in the eye and say, "If you don't stop right now, I'll go to the police."

Body language is important. Square your shoulders, cross your legs, cross your arms across your chest.

Leave. Even if you are in your own home, get out if you think you are in danger. Call the police from a neighbor's or friend's.

SAFETY DEVICES

A WISE WOMAN KNOWS
*Running from danger
is by far the best solution.*

For times when it is difficult to run, make use of security devices that are small enough to carry, such as:

1. Small sharp objects: metal can opener, metal rattail comb or hair pick, metal nail file, wooden pencil sharpened, keys held between two fingers of a fist.

2. Irritating sprays: mace, tear gas, hot pepper, hair spray, or a homemade combination of rubbing alcohol and indelible ink (all blind an assailant temporarily). Choose canisters that open and spray easily for several feet, and with a safety cap.

3. Whistles and alarms.

4. Your voice! "Your best weapon is your voice," say several security experts. "Use it!" Scream, yell, shout.

Remember: No safety device does any good buried in the bottom of a purse. They must be easily accessible.

5. Prayer and rebuke. Some women have discovered that firmly repeating the phrase "I rebuke you in the name of the Lord" over and over has caused a would-be abductor to let them go.

PRACTICE SELF-DEFENSE

Self-defense is "a means of self-preservation that uses weaponless combat to ward off an attacker."[2] There are several methods women can use. A young woman writes in *Seventeen* magazine, "A self-defense course taught me that I'm capable of taking care of myself. If you don't know that about yourself, then you need to learn it's true."[3]

Libraries offer books on self-defense, but it is unlikely that reading a book actually prepares anybody for attack. If you want to take a course in self-defense, bypass traditional martial arts and look for a course specifically designed to teach women to ward off attack. These classes concentrate on training you to respond automatically and powerfully, and to go for the attacker's most vulnerable areas. Community colleges and local YWCAs often offer courses.

Expensive, but highly recommended by police departments, is Model Mugging, a five-day, twenty-five-hour course taught by instructors wearing special armor that permits participants to hit as hard as they would need to in an actual attack situation. For information, call Resources for Personal Empowerment, 1–800–443–KICK.

CHAPTER THIRTEEN

What to Do If You Are the Victim of a Crime

If You are Attacked

Hopefully, you will never be attacked. However, if you are:

1. Trust your instincts. If you can run, do so. Otherwise, try not to be paralyzed by fear. New studies show that a woman who fights back is more likely to be injured but less likely to be raped. Most rape researchers shy away from giving generic advice. They do find, however, that a fast, unexpected aggressive response is more effective than passivity.

2. Use your strengths. One self-defense instructor urges that the most sensible action is to turn sideways and kick backwards (like a mule!), aiming at the attacker's knee or shin. "Most men can block or stop punching blows, but they are not experienced in blocking a kick into the knee or shin. Your leg is stronger than your arm, and even without shoes on you can kick with great force. A relatively small amount of practice will develop your kicking ability surprisingly well."[1]

Weak points are the eyes, the Adam's apple, and the groin. If possible, aim your thumbs or knuckles at his eyes, the side of your hand or your fist at his Adam's apple, and/or your knee to his groin. Stomp his toes or bite him if possible.

3. Act erratically. Convince your attacker that he's got a wild woman on his hands. Scream! Punch! Bite! Kick or knee him in the groin. Spit, bark like a dog, call out, pray loudly.

4. Pray! Ask God for strength and presence of mind.

If You Suspect an Intruder in Your House

Quietly gather the family in one room, shove a chair under the doorknob, and call for help. Avoid confrontation if possible. Do *not* go to investigate, and train children to do the same.

If You Come Home and Find Signs of a Break-In

Go to a neighbor's and call for help. Do *not* go into the house until police arrive.

After a Car Theft

Call the police first, your insurance company second, and a friend, pastor, or coworker third. You do not need to be alone.

When a Purse is Snatched

Do *not* go home alone. The thief has both your address and your keys. Ask the police to go home with you, or call someone to be with you. Call a locksmith immediately. Then, using the list of credit cards you have in your files (See Checklist 4, page 237), call each company to cancel your cards. Until you can change your car locks, arrange to park in someone else's drive or in a locked garage.

If You are Raped

Go to a safe place and call the police immediately. The sooner a rape is reported, the more likely the rapist will be caught. Do not shower, bathe, or douche, as much as you will want to. Do not disturb the clothing you were wearing at the time. Call a friend or a rape crisis center, for you should not be alone. Go to a police station, rape crisis center, or hospital emergency room and tell them you were raped. Be sure that the examining doctor notes all injuries and evaluates you for risk of pregnancy or venereal disease. Finally, write down a description of the person as soon as possible, trying to remember any characteristic accent, use of words, hair part, scars, or traits.

ALWAYS REPORT RAPE OR ATTEMPTED RAPE!

No matter who the man is, report him. Convicted rapists commit an average of sixteen rapes before they are arrested. A man who rapes or tries to rape you may rape others if you do not help stop him!

PART THREE

Putting Other People in the Picture

INTRODUCTION

Almost no woman is utterly alone.

A few are so isolated they seldom see another human being except for forays to the supermarket or church, but most women home alone have active lives. They work, serve on committees, volunteer, socialize, and date. Some have children. Many have a husband who comes and goes. Some even have a husband who comes home every night, but because he regularly disappears into a private world, the wife is still virtually home alone.

This section deals with relationships between women home alone and other people. Chapters deal with:

- how to avoid the emotional traps of consistently painful friendships and unwise romantic entanglements;
- how to maintain a marriage when one spouse is frequently away;
- how to be a more effective single parent through family team building;
- how to evaluate children's illness and cope with minor ones;
- how to help children deal with a father who travels.

Because a woman home alone may be particularly vulnerable to emotional traps, let's begin there.

CHAPTER FOURTEEN

Watch Out for People Traps!

Lord, I never imagined I'd be tempted by another man, but I've been alone so long that I find myself yearning toward kindness and laughter, enthralled by good conversation, charmed by a smile, trembling at a casual touch. Thank you for putting friends like a wall of protection around me tonight. Lead me not into temptation, and deliver me from evil.

Not all people are hedges against isolation for a woman alone. Some people can trap us in relationships that are far worse.

In *Safe People*, Drs. Henry Cloud and John Townsend talk about how to find relationships that are good for us and how to avoid those that aren't. They define "safe people" as those who are good for us because they "truly make us better people by their presence in our lives."[1] Unsafe people, on the other hand, are those whom we cannot trust, who constantly criticize us, who are irresponsible in relationships, or who abandon us.

Cloud and Townsend point out that some people consistently choose unsafe people as friends and lovers. If a stroll through your past reveals a pattern of untrustworthy friends and romantic partners, you might benefit from reading their book and using the accompanying workbook (see the end of this chapter).

Any woman home alone, however, may occasionally choose unwise friends and/or romantic partners, then find herself frustrated when they eat up her time, gnaw around the edges of her self-esteem, and leave her lonelier than before. Here are tips for avoiding relationships that will not be good for you.

AVOID THE WRONG FRIENDS

1. Avoid people who have a list of what you, as a friend, are "supposed" to do. Women's friendships can easily go astray if one thinks, "She owes me a call" and then, when she doesn't call, "She doesn't care." These friends complain if you don't call them as often as they call you, don't always remember their birthdays and special anniversaries, and don't read their minds to know when they are depressed or sick. Gently disengage from these friendships, or insist on new rules. Otherwise, they will drain you.

Real friends forgive one another, keep in touch because they want to and not because they "have" to, and expect each other to have other friends because they know that one friendship cannot meet all needs.

2. Don't confuse those you minister to with friends. It is good to minister to others. However, if you devote a good bit of time to other people and are still lonely, you may be constantly giving while seldom receiving support and comfort yourself. Those who minister to others also need friends. Seek out some people who respect and like you, whom you enjoy and aren't always serving.

3. Take your "safe friends" temperature once in a while. Cloud and Townsend list nine traits that distinguish the interpersonal relationships of safe friends from those of unsafe people.[2] If you spend a good deal of time with other people and still feel lonely or even depressed, evaluate those with whom you spend the most time. How "safe" are your closest associates?

Unsafe People	Safe People
1. Avoid closeness.	1. Enjoy closeness, intimacy.
2. Only concerned about "me."	2. Empathetic to your pain, too.
3. Do not respect your "no" and have no separate life.	3. Respect your "no" and have a life separate from you.

4. Flatter rather than confront.   4. Tell hard truth when needed.
5. Condemn mistakes.   5. Forgive mistakes.
6. Relate as "parent" or   6. Relate as adult to adult.
   "child," but not as "adult."
7. Commit and commit, but   7. Are there when needed.
   don't come through.
8. Negative influence on life.   8. Positive influence on life.
9. Gossip.   9. Keep secrets.

If you find yourself surrounded by friends who are not safe to be with, you may seek other friends or you may try to repair some of those relationships. The last chapter of *Safe People* suggests ways to do that.

AVOID PUTTING ALL YOUR EGGS IN ONE BASKET

Some women home alone try to be utterly independent, coping single-handedly with every crisis and scorning the idea that they need other people for their happiness. When a crisis occurs that they cannot handle, however, they may become emotionally vulnerable to anyone they perceive as stronger than they.

Other women cling desperately to others all the time, terrified they can't make it on their own. Because most people hate to be clung to, these women are vulnerable to anybody who will let them cling.

Neither independence nor dependence is a healthy stance in life, because neither is realistic. Instead . . .

1. Cultivate undependence. An undependent person recognizes that we all have breakdowns on the expressway of life and need somebody to call. But while dependent people always call someone in every crisis—usually the same people—and independent people try *never* to call, undependent people have a variety of persons on whom to call for different needs—and know which crises they can cope with alone.

2. Don't count on any one person—not even a husband— to meet all your needs. Teale said frankly, "When I was a young married woman, I thought my husband was the only thing that mattered. I didn't cultivate friendships with other women. But we started having problems, because I expected him to meet all my needs. I had to learn that he cannot do that."

Some single women are convinced that marriage would end their loneliness, but anyone who has been married knows that married people get lonely, too. Wise couples, even those who are seldom apart, don't find all their happiness in one another. Anthony Storr writes, "It may be our idealization of interpersonal relationships in the West that causes marriage, supposedly the most intimate tie, to be so unstable. If we did not look to marriage as the principle source of happiness, fewer marriages would end in tears."[3]

Women home alone need a variety of friends: friends to dance with and friends to cry with, friends to run with and friends to talk to, friends who like concerts and others who make us laugh. Finding someone with whom to share several facets of life is special. Finding someone who shares many facets is fortunate—and is certainly the basis of a good marriage. However, the only one who can truly share all our life is God.

AVOID UNWISE EMOTIONAL ENTANGLEMENTS

The greatest people trap for a woman home alone may be sexual. After my husband moved and left me home alone, I read in a beauty parlor magazine: "People with active sex lives are less anxious, violent, hostile, or likely to blame others for misfortunes. Happy lovers make the best spouses."

My reaction as a woman without a spouse around? "Thanks a lot!" What is a woman home alone supposed to do?

1. Stay busy. Hymn-writer Isaac Watts once wrote, "For Satan finds some mischief still for idle hands to do." It may make us smile, but it is true: the busier we are, the less time and energy we have for fruitless imaginings or unhealthy activities.

2. Avoid unhealthy people and situations. Paula recommends: "Don't hang around with desperately lonely women. Also, don't read romance novels or hang around temptation spots. If you are on a diet, you don't hang around Baskin Robbins! When I feel lonely, I don't spend time with people or go to places that make me feel more lonely or tempt me to do things I shouldn't to ease my loneliness."

3. Don't confuse neediness with love. Lonely women are vulnerable to what I call Country Music Love. Country music commonly has three themes:

1. "I'm so lonely I could die."
2. "Now I've got a new love who's going to make everything all right."
3. "My lover let me down. Where did it all go wrong?"

It makes good music, but it's a dreadful way to live your life!

Love is not merely chemistry that makes you tingle. Love is not somebody who takes all your problems on his shoulders. Love is not somebody else who will run your life. Love is not what you feel at midnight after a deeply intimate conversation or too many drinks.

Real love is described in 1 Corinthians 13:4–7:

> Love is patient, love is kind. It does not envy, it does not boast, it is not proud. It is not rude, it is not self-seeking, it is not easily angered, it keeps no record of wrongs. Love does not delight in evil but rejoices in the truth. It always protects, always trusts, always hopes, always perseveres.

Love is a mature, growing relationship between two people who each know who they are and how to be whole without anybody else. Love is for grown-ups.

Love is also about sex with commitment. Barbara Holland writes: "Even the least religious or superstitious among us now feel uneasily that something out there doesn't approve of sex with strangers, and whatever that something is, it has a lot more clout than our mothers."[4]

Remember how the 1 Corinthians passage begins? "Love is patient." If you are single, lonely, and think you are falling in love, give it time to ripen. If it's real love, it won't go away.

4. Lean on your friends. Meg Woodson asks, "How do we avoid making foolish choices in the area of our love lives? We tend to think of love as a very private matter and that a woman's taste in men is very personal. But we need to get away from this kind of individualistic thinking. When it comes to something as serious as marriage, we desperately need the advice and counsel of others, especially family and friends. If they are questioning our choice, then so ought we."[5]

See Adultery for What it is: Wrong.

Every woman ever drawn toward an adulterous relationship feels that hers is different, special, somehow purer than the sordid relationships other people have. Few are able to see the pain they can cause not only themselves, but a circle of family and friends around them. A woman tempted to commit adultery needs to know she isn't the first woman to feel this way.

I once met with a group of young wives in which almost everyone had, at least once, felt attracted to another man. Sharing lessons learned from those experiences strengthened all our marriages. We concluded that feeling attraction and battling it gives us wisdom to share with others. Feeling attraction and yielding to it just complicates our lives.

A wife I interviewed for this book recalls, "When my husband was gone a good bit, I got attracted to a man who had communication skills my husband didn't have. The best thing I ever did in our marriage was sit my husband down when he got home and say, 'I'm finding myself attracted to another man because he talks to me and listens when I talk.' My husband was able to see that, and we've worked on that ever since."

Another wife advises, "Don't put yourself in a situation where you are tempted. I once served on a church committee with a man whom I saw more often than I saw my husband. I began to look forward to his calls, and I made up excuses to call him. Finally I realized I had to get off that committee and remove myself from temptation. And I needed to make more effort to keep in touch with my husband while he was out of town. We needed to get connected and stay connected."

A WISE WOMAN KNOWS
Temptation isn't sin.
It's yielding to temptation that is sin.

A third said thoughtfully, "To commit adultery, you don't have to give your body to somebody else. You can just give him the best of you—your thoughts, daydreams, and your greatest kindness."

A fourth wife said, "My husband has a friend who travels as much as he does. They hold one another accountable, even to ask some of the hard questions like, 'Are you being faithful to your wife?'" Wives of men who are frequently gone might hold one another similarly accountable.

IN CONCLUSION

Emotional traps can ensnare any woman home alone in the shape of relationships with unsafe people, isolation that leads to dependence on too few people for happiness or help in crisis, and even sexual temptation born of loneliness and boredom.

The best way to avoid those traps is to find safe friends with whom to share different parts of life, to stay busy, and become undependent.

A Declaration of Undependence

1. I am a whole person whether I am with someone else or not.
2. My happiness does not depend on another person.
3. I will not expect one person to meet all my needs, nor will I permit another person to expect that of me.

Suggested Further Reading

Cloud, Dr. Henry, and Dr. John Townsend. *Safe People: How to Find Relationships That Are Good for You and Avoid Those That Aren't.* Grand Rapids: Zondervan, 1995. Helps identify persons who are not helpful as friends and intimates and those who are. Comes with a workbook for personal reflection.

Russianoff, Penelope. *Why Do I Think I Am Nothing Without a Man?* New York: Bantam, 1982. Well-known counselor helps women build self-esteem as a way to break out of consistently harmful relationships.

CHAPTER FIFTEEN

*When Does a Wife Not Feel Like a Wife?**

Lord, I've had enough of going to parties alone, children's recitals alone, church alone, and bed alone. I am especially tired of hearing him say how much he misses us when I'm here trying to hold everything together. It's hard to sympathize with him on days like today. It all seems like his fault.

With so much attention being paid to problems of the family these days, it is odd that so little is being said about one of the greatest stresses on many marriages: a traveling spouse.

Weekly they sally forth to sell, manage, consult, patrol, police, heal, transport goods and people, wage war, minister to others, or spread the gospel. They are to be found most weekdays gathered around continental breakfasts in expensive hotels, eating expense account lunches, and passing lonely evenings in hotel rooms or bars.

They are the pampered darlings of a nation that gives them wide airplane seats and hotel suites with three telephones, bathroom television, and a Jacuzzi. They are also lonely outcasts—

_____
*When she's a woman home alone.

seldom anywhere three nights in a row, limited to superficial relationships, too many restaurant meals and too little exercise. They are under constant pressure to work harder, and doomed to grow old or die young with only glimpses of their children throughout rapidly disappearing childhoods. And although they may worry about their families back home, social structures increasingly require them to yo-yo between home and far-flung business opportunities.

During the Gulf War, women combatants raised acutely the poignant issue of what happens to separated families. As more women travel in their work they, too, are beginning to raise social awareness about damage done to families by current ways of doing business—and they are precipitating some changes. One national consulting firm has promised employees they will never have to leave home earlier than 7 A.M. on Mondays and will always get home Friday evening.

That's a beginning.

Most travelers, however, are still men. Their wives make up a major segment of women home alone—with all the restrictions of marriage and few of the privileges. Just like their unmarried sisters, they maintain a house and car, keep up with both personal and family friendships, and often raise children solo, all the while wondering, "Is this what marriage is supposed to be like?"

Lori says, "My husband loves his job, and I'm glad he does. But why should we pretend it's normal when it's not?"

MISSING LITTLE THINGS THAT MEAN A LOT

"Missing one another. That's the hardest part." Wives said it again and again in interviews. Some, like Lori, miss sharing the most important moments of marriage: "He was away when our daughter was born. He left in May when I was six months pregnant, and he came home in November to a three-month-old."

Other wives miss companionship. Jill said wistfully, "When he's gone, I miss our time together in the evening. We usually sit and talk and unwind at night, and figure out how to deal with daily issues. I miss that."

107

Traveling husbands miss things, too. A warm foot on the other side of the bed when they wake at night. Somebody to hug when they have a great day—or to hold them when they have a bad one. Talking or just watching TV together to unwind. Going to church suppers or midweek movies. Family jokes. Funny events that aren't so funny secondhand. Burying the family dog. One traveling husband told me, "You never get used to it. You just don't."

Allison also wonders, "How can he develop friendships when he's gone all the time? He has pleasant relationships with men at parties, but when he's home, mostly he concentrates on the kids. He plays with the boys, and since he's here every weekend, he is here for most of their games. But when does he have time to build friendships with other men?"

Some women take the traveling in stride. When I called June to ask if I could interview her about being alone, she said, "I'm not alone more than anybody else."

"But isn't your husband a pilot for an international cargo company?" I asked. "Doesn't he fly several nights every week?"

I could almost see her shrug at her end of the phone. "Sure, he's gone a lot of nights. But most times he gets home at six in the morning, about the time I'm getting up to go to work. We have breakfast, he sleeps while I'm working, and we have our evenings together." This from a woman whose husband flies all over the western hemisphere!

Yet she is right. A husband who arrives in time for breakfast is home more than a graduate student who spends most nights haunting the library. Jean remembers, "The greatest time of stress in our marriage was law school. We never saw each other. I had two young kids and no car, no career. Over fifty percent of our classmates who were married before law school got divorced."

Oddly, while our fast-track society puts enormous pressures on families by separating them, few analysts blame the policies of corporations, institutions, the military, or graduate schools for the much-touted decline of the American family. Apparently, nobody sees the connection. Even sociologists who study travelers and stress devote little attention to their wives.

Is that because wives home alone are so invisible? They show up at church or social functions with a husband beside them, so the world conveniently assumes they, like other wives, have a steady companion, coparent, and somebody with whom to share a crisis.

Yet wives home alone need the same support systems as unmarried women—and help in maintaining marriages, as well. The following suggestions for maintaining marriages when a husband travels come from wives who deal with the issue on a regular basis.

STAYING IN TOUCH

Studies of infants show that those who feel securely loved are less likely to be distressed when left with strangers for some stretch of time. A study of families with one traveling member would probably show the same thing: they need to give one another *big* doses of love and security. That means staying in touch.

For Trips of a Few Days

1. Call frequently! Both Jean and Allison said, "We talk an hour every night. In fact, we have more conversation when he's gone than we do when he's here and we both get busy with other things." Teale points out that "Lots of times there's nothing to say on our end except 'We're all here, bored stiff, getting homework done and piano practiced.' Still, it's good to have him call."

2. Tuck encouraging notes in your husband's suitcase.

3. While he's away, keep a journal. Lynn said, "When Bas comes back from a three-week trip, we follow each other around for days, talking. A journal helps us remember what we didn't want to forget at the time."

4. Travel with your husband enough to have some idea of what he does when away.

5. Tuck a family picture in his suitcase.

For Long Trips

1. Send pictures of family events to the traveler.

2. Send tapes of family members' voices.

3. *Write frequently.* Lori said, "I write him almost every day. You know you are saying the same things over and over, but it doesn't really matter. You also daydream in letters about what you'll do when he comes home."

4. *Send little things that remind him of home:* his favorite candy, pictures of the baby or friends, new music you think he'll like.

TIPS FOR A TRAVELING SPOUSE

1. *Phone home often.* Set a specific time to call so you'll both be available.

2. *ALWAYS leave numbers where you can be reached.* Suzanne said, "The worst thing that's happened to us since he went on the road was when I desperately needed to reach him and couldn't. I was terrified! After that, he always leaves numbers where I can reach him, and we established a time for him to call each day, so I don't ever have to feel that desperate again."

Judy's husband's father died while he was on the road. "I thought I'd never get him. Finally I just prayed a desperate prayer. God nudged him to return to his motel room in mid-morning, which he almost never does, and there was my message to call me at once. Otherwise, he wouldn't have gotten the message until late that night."

3. *While away, keep a journal:* decisions, insights, events worth remembering, difficulties, personal joys and hurts, and funny happenings to share with the family when you get home.

4. *Make sure the family has a good picture of you.* Several wives mentioned that they do not have a recent picture of their spouse. Without being macabre, we take a risk whenever we leave home. Keep photographs up-to-date. It's an easy thing to do for your family.

If You'll be Gone a Week or More

1. *Leave a taped message for small children.* Goodnight tapes were mentioned as especially good for preschool children to listen to each night before bed. They won't mind listening to the same one again and again.

2. *Bring home presents!* It says to the family, "Even if I had to be away, I was thinking of how precious you are to me."

3. *Make a photojournal.* The family would like to see where you've been.

4. *Leave something behind for each family member.* Lynn remembers: "In our early years of doing this, Bas left us cards and letters to open every three days."

RELATING TO THE EXTENDED FAMILY

1. *Let the family help as much as you feel comfortable with.* Lori's brother, who lives nearby, asks her to call him when she'll be driving home late and finally gets home. When her husband was at sea, her mother shared in the birth of her baby. She says, "I have a lot of family support, which makes things easier."

Lauren, however, pointed out that dependence on one's birth family is not always ideal. "We live next door to my sister, and my parents live two houses away. My husband doesn't worry about me when he's gone, and doesn't bother to call frequently, because he assumes Dad will take care of any emergencies that arise. But I hesitate to call on my family for every little thing. That doesn't feel very grown-up." Lauren, therefore, only calls on them for occasional child care and house or car emergencies.

2. *Expect in-laws to be both a blessing and an additional burden.* Karen's mother-in-law also had a traveling husband, so "she sent flowers and extra money for me to have a special time while he was gone." Sue's mother-in-law, however, "managed five kids alone much of the time, so she never thought it was a big deal. It was harder for me. I didn't grow up like that."

Lori points out, "It's hard for me to keep up with his family when he's at sea. I want to keep them up-to-date, particularly about the baby, but it's another whole set of people to keep up with, call, write, and visit."

When couples are having marriage problems, in-law relationships may be especially awkward when one spouse travels. A divorced wife said sadly, "I couldn't tell our parents that we were having problems. It felt disloyal. But they were stunned when we broke up."

DEALING WITH RESENTMENTS

A wife home alone can develop many resentments:

- resentment that the job takes him away so much,
- resentment that the job places him in danger,
- resentment that he doesn't understand how much extra work his job causes her,
- resentment that he eats on an expense account while she eats peanut butter sandwiches or microwave dinners,
- resentment that he comes home weary and drained, tired of restaurant meals, just when the family wants to eat out.

Suzanne said frankly, "I think we all have to deal with feelings that his job comes first and his family comes after that."

How do wives deal with that?

1. Admit the resentment and find ways to deal with it. "Sometimes I just go out to the beach and scream!" said one wife. Others talk with a counselor or pastor. And August makes sure the family has fun, too. "The kids and I do a lot of special things when he's away. After all, he's having adventures. Why shouldn't we?"

2. Remind yourself why he is away. Suzanne, after admitting she sometimes feels his job comes first, added, "I try to remember why he works so hard. It seems like the more successful he gets, the higher we both want him to go, so the more he has to be on the road."

Lynn, who has traveled with her husband on several mission trips, said, "I have seen how valuable his work is, and the women his organization serves. Their lives are so difficult; they keep me in perspective. I rejoice that he's doing something to improve their lives."

3. Look for ways to help him understand YOUR side of his traveling. Suzanne no longer has one resentment other wives expressed: resentment that her husband doesn't realize how much stress his being away creates for her. "I sprained my ankle and couldn't walk. He had to stay home for a week and do everything around here by himself, without any help from me. After that, I heard him telling a friend, 'Hey, Suzanne's job's not that easy either!'"

That kind of respect goes a long way.

If you don't want to sprain an ankle, could you keep a log for several weeks to show what you have done with your time? Or send this book along on his next trip?

4. See yourselves as an at-home/traveling partnership. When Lynn's husband first considered traveling, their children were twelve and eight. "We were concerned whether this job would mean we would sacrifice the family to do the job. Neither of us wanted that to happen. We decided we needed to look for models of other traveling families that had thrived. One woman who had already gone through what I was about to take on was the wife of the man who had the job until my husband took it. She raised four children, and I respected the children and the obvious love they all have for their parents. There seemed to be no bitterness in the kids, no resentment. So I asked their mother how she had done so well.

"She told me that from the beginning, they had made her husband's ministry the family ministry. His part was to go and do; their part was to joyfully release him and be obedient and cooperate. When he was home, he was fully present to the children and his wife. Each time he left, he told each child, 'In your obedience to the Lord and love for me, cooperate with the family.'"

"Whenever my husband has a trip coming up," Lynn continued, "he talks it over with me before he agrees to go. I've never told him not to go, but it makes me feel a part of his decision."

What difference might it make in any family if everybody's work was seen as family work, and the whole family respectfully invited to share in it?

MAINTAINING A DELICATE BALANCE

Wives who spend much of their time alone walk a tightrope between self-reliance and partnership—making complete lives for themselves, yet trying to keep their lives flexible and open enough to let their husband in as one who belongs, not merely visits.

Or picture them at one end of an old-fashioned two-person saw—sometimes with a partner to help pull, but sometimes having to figure out how to pull the whole thing alone. At times they must thrust forward, other times fall back. It is a most delicate role.

Martha, whose husband travels in sales and is gone almost every week, said frankly, "I'm so used to doing things by myself that when he's home a week, it's awkward. I have all these things I'm supposed to do—choir, Bible study, stuff at the girls' schools. But if I go out in the evening, I feel like I'm abandoning him. Am I supposed to readjust my whole schedule just because he's not going on the road that week?"

Allison reflects, "My strong support system bothers my spouse. When he's in town, he tends to get jealous of the women friends I have. 'You don't need me,' he tells me. The truth is, after all these years of his traveling, he's right. I want him, but I don't need him. I've arranged my life around his being gone. It never occurred to me that would bother him, but he has said several times, 'All I am to you is a paycheck.'"

Therefore, it is healthy to frequently remind yourself and your spouse that

- you appreciate the advantages he provides the family through his work, and
- even if you've arranged your life around his being gone, and have your week full of good things to do, you enjoy his company more than that of anybody else, and look forward to his return.

COMING HOME WISDOM FOR A WIFE ALONE

Having a traveling husband come home can be as hard as having him leave! Here are a few tips to make the return home easier:

1. Don't unload everything as soon as he comes in the door. "That's hard," Suzanne admits. "When he gets home, I've been home with a two-year-old for three or four days, and I want to meet him at the door with 'The toilet's blocked up, and the kid's been a brat!' We have learned to deal with that by him calling before he leaves to drive home. I tell him everything that's been going on, especially any problems around here. That way, he's prepared and can think about how to solve them on his drive back, and I've already unloaded."

If you can't unload ahead of his return, write down what you want to talk about and save it for the next day. Who wants to come home to be hit with a gunnysack of problems?

2. Don't expect him to want to go out once he gets in. While wives—especially those with small children—may yearn to go out and do something, husbands home from the road want to stay home and putter. As Allison said wryly, "Going out to dinner is no big treat to somebody who's been on the road all week. Restaurants lose their charm."

Wives can solve that by eating out, too, while he's away. Invite single friends to meet for lunch or dinner and a movie, or meet other single moms and their kids for dinner. Put the grown-ups at one table and the children at another, and make it an event.

Allison has a good meal and a clean house waiting for her husband's return. "Those are very restful for him."

Judy has learned: "When my husband comes home Friday, he's tired. We turn off the television that evening and talk. I've also gotten more considerate about getting stuff done during the week so he doesn't have to."

3. Don't expect him to want to socialize right away. He may yearn for solitude if he's been in meetings and crowds. When Teale's husband came home from India, she planned a huge party for three days after he came home. "He was so mad!" she remembers. "I was trying to do something nice for him, but he hadn't recovered from jet lag yet, and he told me, 'The last thing I want to see is people.' I had thirty people coming over. I learned he needs time to recover when he gets back from a long trip."

June said, "He's away from our daughter so much that we plan our life around her social activities when he's home rather than trying to have a social life of our own. After all, she'll be gone soon enough."

On the other hand, he may want a life of his own once he gets home. Lauren reflected, "One hard thing for me to accept is that when he is home for a weekend, he wants to go fishing with his buddies. I don't like him being away, but I do know why he's away and we're reaping the benefits, so I've come to accept it. But when he finally has a day off and decides to go fishing with some guys—it hurts. I know he needs time to have fun, but I feel left out." She added practically, "I keep reminding myself that I get to do what I want to all week. The only time he gets to do what he wants is when he's home."

4. Give a traveler time on both ends of a trip. Lynn said, "When he makes a big trip, we lose two extra weeks: the week before he goes and the week after he comes back. Before he goes, he's pressured with getting all the loose ends at work and home tied up. After he's back, he has to catch up and do all the closure stuff from his trip. So a three-week trip is really five weeks, counting two weeks of preoccupation and emotional distance. I have had to learn that when he drops his luggage in the hall, he is not 'home and now ours.' I know I still have to fill emotional gaps in the family those days."

5. Prepare for minor adjustments. "He'll get in bed at night and want to read, and I'm used to turning out lights and going to sleep. Suddenly I have a light back on again." Or "He'll leave a suitcase packed on the floor for a week." Or "He wants me to run errands for him—like I don't have things of my own to do."

In group interviews, wives seemed both to enjoy and to take comfort from sharing those stories and learning that other wives have similar problems. Wives of traveling men really need to get together from time to time. They have so much in common!

COMING HOME WISDOM FOR A RETURNING HUSBAND

Most wives try to make their husband's transition as easy as possible, but husbands need to help. After all, your return is an adjustment for everybody.

1. Let her know when you're coming, if possible. Lauren said, "I used to hate waiting for him to get in. The meal would be ruined, or I'd worry that he'd had an accident. Then he bought a cellular phone. Now he calls on the road to say, 'I'm on my way and should be there by—' whenever. I don't have to wait and wait for him to walk in."

2. Anticipate some edginess on both your parts. A wife who's been "head of the household" may feel her territory and authority are under attack. A husband is returning to a life, shared jokes, and experiences he's missed. "Sometimes I feel like a visitor," one husband told me. "My family's life is like a movie everybody has already seen but me."

A wife voiced a similar thought. "As bad as it sounds, the day he comes home always messes up our schedule. We're used to simple meals and doing things at a certain time, and then suddenly we all have to adjust our schedules around him."

3. Don't criticize decisions she's made while you were gone! One wife complained, "He says I always spend more money when he's not here. It can be a five-dollar purchase, but he'll say, 'You spent this for that?' I have to justify so many decisions I've made. If he'd been home and I'd done the same thing, he wouldn't have said a word, but he always comes home criticizing me." Ouch!

4. Accept that if she's carrying the home-front load for two, some things won't get done. "My husband is always calling and giving me instructions," says my neighbor, who is home alone with a tiny baby. "He wants me to run an errand, or take his clothes to the cleaner's, or take back his library books. He doesn't realize how much I have to do because he is away. Everything falls on me!"

A working wife sighed. "He doesn't understand why I can't clean the house before he gets home. He doesn't realize that it takes all the time I have just to keep things running smoothly while he's gone. Major cleaning is one of the things that just has to wait."

WISDOM FOR BOTH PARTNERS

Key, a veteran Coast Guard wife, advises, "We need to remember that while we wives have to do a lot of adjusting when our husbands return, so do they. It's hard on them when their kids don't recognize them when they get home. It's hard to feel like we cope so well when they are gone that we don't really need them. With all the coming and going, I find it's helpful to keep a sense of humor."

COUNTING THE BLESSINGS

While there are undeniable drawbacks to having a traveling husband, some wives also see benefits. June, whose husband flies at night and gets home in the morning, suggested, "I probably see more of my husband than a lot of wives do. We have evenings together, we have most weekends together, and when he's not flying, he's there all the time. He does a lot of our housework in those times. He likes to vacuum." (No, she does not lend him out.)

Allison pointed out that because her husband calls each night, "we actually get more quality time together when he's gone than when he's here. When he's here the children want time with him and we are both involved in projects. But our time on the phone each evening is *our* time."

Sue and Karen both found that letter writing can bring couples closer. Sue said, "In our first year of marriage we only saw each other about six months, so we got to know each other better through letters." Karen agreed. "My husband's such a tease in person that I didn't know he was a poet until he was away and wrote me letters."

The most frequently mentioned blessing was frequent flier miles. "If my husband didn't travel," Martha said with a laugh, "I'd never get to visit my brother."

A GOOD LAST WORD

Sue concluded her interview with this wisdom for other wives alone: "Tell him often that you need him. Not because you can't manage things alone, but because you have a partnership. Sure I am independent and strong, but I need him emotionally. I need the love we share. I can't imagine life without him. The absences have only helped our romance stay alive!"

CHAPTER SIXTEEN

Alone
—With Two Children,
Three Gerbils, and a Dog

Lord, at his class play, my son was the only marcher in "76 Trombones"
with gray pants. He swears he told me he needed white ones "the other
night," but I don't think so. What if he did and I just forgot? I'm nearly
crazy, Lord, with all their end-of-school activities and my own work.
I try to keep up, but there's so much to keep up with! Help me not to
mess up on anything important the children will remember or regret.

No matter how much she loves them, children complicate
life for a woman home alone. Children require constant encouraging,
disciplining, listening to, feeding, and driving. Small ones need
diapering, older ones need help with homework. Yet mothers alone
have no backup—either to give them a breather or to help make
and enforce family rules. Mothers alone with adolescents also have
nobody to remind them that they aren't really dumber, squarer, and
more out of sync with the modern world than anybody else's parents.

Given that a mother alone has so much responsibility, how
can she make life more pleasant and manageable?

STRUCTURE LIFE TO WORK FOR YOU

What works in a two-parent family doesn't always work when Mother is the only parent, when children shuttle between two parents, or when Dad travels in his work. Children may have to learn to change gears—to adjust to different rules and expectations between two divorced parents or, if Dad travels, to a looser schedule when he's away. However, some structure is important for the sake of your children and your own sanity.

Exactly what structure? Only you can determine that. Nobody is as "expert" on what works in your family as you. Here, however, are a few guidelines suggested by women who have faced similar situations:

1. See your family as a team. Any family works best if all members feel they are a part of a cohesive whole. People need time to explain what's going on in their lives and call on other family members for prayer or help. One good way to build a family team is to have family meetings. Some families meet weekly, others meet monthly or quarterly. The important thing is to develop a family forum in which to discuss housekeeping routines, what you want to do together, how things are working, and what changes might make the family work better.

Guidelines for a Family Meeting[1]

1. Keep distractions to a minimum. Turn off the television and telephone and put infants and toddlers to bed.

2. Decide at the beginning how long you will meet. Half an hour? An hour?

3. Make up an agenda by asking "What do we need to talk about?" Rate items A (very important or urgent), B (less important or urgent), and C (unimportant, not urgent).

4. Deal with A items first.

5. Listen to everyone, without belittling or ignoring anyone. Give family members time to initiate ideas, actions, and solutions. (Parents need to

remember to listen, listen, listen, and be thick-skinned when listening to complaints.)

6. Set goals for a coming week, both for individuals and the family, and write down.

7. Post goals in a prominent place.

8. Set a time for the next family meeting.

9. End on time, even if you must carry over agenda items for the next meeting.

10. Afterwards, have fun together—play a game, make popcorn and lemonade.

2. Cooperate in household chores. One reason some women do too much is that their children do too little. Mothers alone, especially, need to involve children in household responsibilities. Not only does that teach children skills they will eventually need as adults, but it provides welcome relief for a mother who has been doing it all.

Linda, a single mother, explained another reason why children in one-parent households need to help out. "We had a traumatic divorce. I felt so sorry for my daughter and what she was going through that I hated to ask her to work around the house. I felt guilty for making her do chores. I wasn't doing her any favors, though. It's very important for children in single-parent families to work around the house. It not only gives them a sense of responsibility that they are a part of the family unit, but also gives them a sense of security because they are helping to stabilize the situation."[2]

If you have never expected your children to do housework, and have not considered what adult skills they need to learn before they are able to leave home, read my book *Do I Have To? What to Do About Children Who Do Too Little Around the House*, in which parents, educators, counselors, and personnel directors explain why we need to teach our children household skills for their own sake, how to start them off, how to teach skills instead of chores, and how to deal with rebellion.

Doreen said, "One thing that helped with my two sons when my husband was away so much was that we were a family and all in the situation together. They had regular chores. I taught all the time, and they knew they had to help—it was important to all of us."

3. *Only set rules you are willing to enforce.* When things get out of hand, it's easy to lay down a long list of firm rules and expect that by naming the laws, we will magically persuade our children to obey them. Children, however, learn early how to test parents to determine which rules they really will enforce! Since a mother alone has no backup system to enforce rules when she is tired, grumpy, or absent, she does well to have fewer rules and stick with those. Some mothers post the rules on the refrigerator, so everybody remembers exactly what they are.

Doreen said whimsically, "We had the golden rule around our house: The one with the gold makes the rules. Some things were democratic, but I decided which. The more responsible the children became, the more freedom they got."

4. *Teach your children to make wise choices.* To repeat something from chapter 2, making good choices is a habit and making bad choices is a habit. Children who are from a very young age permitted to make choices *and expected to live with the consequences* habitually make better choices.

Children's choices begin with food and clothing, then extend to when they shall do homework, when they go to bed, who their friends are, what they do with leisure time, and finally—when they start driving—where they go and what they do when they are on their own.

As we help our children learn to make wise choices, we keep in mind what our job is as parents: to help our children out of our lives and into responsible adulthood.

5. *Deal early and firmly with deadly issues.* Many choices our children are offered these days are dangerous, even deadly. One mother said, "I'd rather my child made all her bad mistakes while she's at home, before the consequences get fatal."

Proverbs 1:10–19 gives principles for helping a child make good choices about important moral issues:

- *Set out what is likely to happen:* "My son, if sinners entice you, do not give in to them."
- *Outline what the enticers will promise:* "If we waylay some harmless soul, we will get all sorts of valuable things and fill our houses with plunder."
- *Point out clearly what is far more likely to happen instead:* "These men lie in wait for their own blood; they waylay only themselves. Such is the end of all who go after ill-gotten gain; it takes away the lives of those who get it."

If you have a hard time knowing how to relate consequences to poor moral choices, you may want to provide a "field trip" or volunteer opportunity for your child, or for you and the child together. If your child is

- Driving recklessly—visit an emergency room on a Saturday night.
- Experimenting with drugs—visit a drug-rehab center.
- Flirting with breaking the law—visit inmates at the county jail.
- Possibly sexually promiscuous—visit a local AIDS hospice.

One mother, faced with a daughter who wanted nothing after high school except to have a baby, took in a foster infant. A dose of genuine, unrelenting child care sent that teenager to both college and graduate school!

We mothers cannot make our children good, but we can hold up a clear mirror showing likely consequences of unwise behavior. A child learns more from seeing consequences than from a thousand motherly naggings.

THE TOUGHEST ISSUE: WISE DISCIPLINE

Discipline is hard enough when two parents are at home. Is it easier, or harder, when there's only one parent at home? Both.

It is easier to discipline without having another parent disagree or question what we've done. But no matter how much we want to always be reasonable and wise, there are days when weariness or temper overwhelm us. Thank God, children who know we love them and try most of the time to be wise and consistent parents will often graciously overlook occasional lapses. However, here are a few guidelines for more consistent discipline:

1. No must mean NO! It's easy when tired to fling out "no's" without bothering to listen to a request or think it over. But if we say "no" and really mean "well, maybe" or "if you whine or scream long enough, I'll let you," our children become petty tyrants who throw tantrums in grocery stores and escalate both their decibels and their demands as they get older. Meanwhile, we are run ragged and stay angry a lot of the time without knowing why.

A WISE WOMAN KNOWS
If you believe in peace at any price,
the price goes higher and higher.

Of course we may sometimes change our minds if a child presents a polite, calm, reasoned argument; we are wiser, however, to usually listen to their side of the issue before we speak, and then "simply let [our] 'Yes' be 'Yes' and our 'No,' 'No'" (Matthew 5:37).

2. Discipline gently. The apostle Paul wisely instructed parents in Ephesians 6:4, "Do not provoke your children to anger"(RSV). He doesn't say not to be firm with them, but we don't need to use a cannon when a water pistol will do.

3. Involve older children in making the rules AND setting the consequences for not keeping the rules. Anyone is more likely to keep rules he understands and agrees with, and children have a keen sense of what's "fair." Listen to them. Children who help make family rules and help set consequences for disobedience are far more likely to keep the rules.

IF I HAD TIME I'D HAVE A BREAKDOWN

"No relief" is a common complaint when mothers alone describe their situation.

- No relief from making decisions alone and wondering if they are the right ones.
- No relief from answering questions.

- No relief from being the only parent to get up in the night with a sick child and up in the morning to put another on a six-thirty bus.
- No relief from having to deal with all the misbehavior, all the crises, all the learning disabilities, all the teacher conferences.
- No relief from mountains of laundry, thousands of meals, sinkfuls of dishes, and spats.

"Late afternoon and early evening are miserable," Brenda says. "Mom is tired, junior is hungry and bored, and there's no relief pitcher coming on the mound around 6:00 P.M. Evenings when my husband was away were not my finest moments as a mom."

"When I was a teacher and had my evenings free," Lauren recalls wistfully, "I really enjoyed being alone. I could do what I wanted. Now, after being home with a three-year-old all day, an evening by myself isn't much fun. I'd like to have an adult to talk to."

On my bedroom mirror I've had a quote from Erma Bombeck for so long that the ink is faded and I don't know which book it came from. She could have been speaking for any mother raising children alone: "I'm a woman who's got it all. If I had any more, I'd be in intensive care."

How does a mother alone avoid a nervous breakdown? Here are some of their suggestions:

1. Know you are not alone. More than any other women, mothers alone need to seek out others who understand. Brenda says one thing that kept her sane was "a standing invitation to have dinner on Wednesday nights with a woman whose husband traveled more than mine. She had figured out some great no-fuss dinners, and I brought food over at least once. Doing it every week made a big difference to me. It was something to look forward to."

Note how much Brenda appreciated the invitation. Note also that another woman home alone initiated the invitation and set limits to make it pleasant for both families.

Mothers alone may hesitate to call on others for parenting advice, support, and relief because they don't like to admit they need help. "I feel like such a wimp," Lauren admits ruefully. But think again. Twelve million single mothers and millions more with husbands who travel know *exactly* what you are going through.

Where do you find them? At sports team practices, school events and PTA meetings, church school classes. Call your church secretary and ask who else in the congregation is raising children alone or frequently alone. Announce in a church or community newsletter that you want to get together with other mothers alone. You may be surprised to find how many others think they are the "only one" in this situation.

"But don't let getting together turn into gripe sessions," several mothers warn. "Gripes have a way of growing, and you feel worse afterwards than you did before." They recommend that mothers alone agree to seek advice from one another, share a success for each failure you discuss, and pray together over issues you can't seem to solve.

2. Arrange for occasional breaks from child care. A friend who got divorced from a husband who had traveled a lot told me wryly, "There are some advantages to divorce. At least now I get alternate weekends free."

Mothers alone without that "advantage" have to seek other alternatives. MOPS (Mothers of Preschoolers) chapters in some congregations offer a regular "haven for frazzled nerves" through caring, sharing, and fun while preschoolers are in a supervised program. To find or start a local chapter, contact MOPS International, Inc., 1311 South Clarkson Street, Denver, CO 80210, 303–733–5353.

Other mothers of preschoolers arrange weekly play groups or regular swaps. Mothers of older children rely on scouts, a church youth group, or special lessons to provide occasional breaks. Two single moms decided not only to carpool for church youth group, but to take turns feeding *and* driving on that evening—giving each mom two free evenings a month.

Some moms rely on extended family. If you are fortunate enough to have family near enough to call on, sit down and talk frankly about how much care they feel comfortable giving and how much you feel comfortable asking for. Getting that on the table is far better than one party feeling guilty or the other feeling imposed on.

If you don't have family, can you budget for an occasional short-term sitter so you can pursue a personal interest? Several times when our boys were small I hired a teenager to keep the children at our home while I wrote. Our rule was, "Don't bother me if you can handle it, but I'm here if you need me." Look for someone too young for a work permit but mature enough to be responsible.

Teale's boys are old enough to leave alone in the evening, but "while they will stay alone for a few hours when their dad and I go out to dinner, if he's gone and I want to go out with a friend, they object, 'But Daddy's not here.' Friends invite the boys over sometimes when my husband's away. That's when I call a woman friend to go to a movie or dinner."

Whatever it takes, a mother alone needs to give herself an occasional break.

3. Give yourself deliberate treats. Get a new hairstyle, read a new book, invite a friend to the movies, or sit on your patio with a long cold drink. "Sometimes," Karen says, "I take one of our five children out for a special dinner. We get all dressed up, go to a 'real' restaurant, and have a leisurely meal with conversation. Both of us enjoy the time away from the others."

4. Seek solitude. As we discussed in chapter 6, every woman needs some time alone. Your children also need for you to have some time alone. Keep repeating those two truths over and over until you believe them! Beth, a mother of four whom I interviewed for an earlier book, said she used to take a "prayer break" when things overwhelmed her. "Some days," she can remember now with a laugh, "my children would beg, 'Mama, go take another prayer break!'"

A WISE WOMAN KNOWS
Changes of attitude
are facilitated by solitude.[3]

5. Involve your family in a larger family. If you are not already part of a congregation, seek one. Not only to build your faith, but because both a mother alone and her children need contact with other families. Key says, "I couldn't have made it without my various churches. Everywhere we move, we get involved in a church. I join a choir and find a Sunday school class. When my husband is gone, they become my family."

You can also *volunteer* as a family. Karen's family has a puppet ministry they take to nursing homes, churches, and special events. One outgrowth of that ministry: her college daughter is majoring in elementary education with an emphasis on puppetry.

6. Consider sharing your space. Sometimes two single mothers decide to move in together. Others offer a college student a room in exchange for child care and housekeeping. Draw up a written contract together defining responsibilities expected and what else is agreed upon: will you share food or buy separately? who cleans which rooms? who pays utility and telephone bills? what about guests, especially overnight guests? If you can live up to your contract, you may find this arrangement makes life easier for everybody.

IN CONCLUSION

Being a mother alone is a tough job no matter what age the children. Moms alone need one another for support, advice, and relief. They need occasional breaks from children and the load. They need treats, they need solitude, they need a wider family.

Mothers I interviewed offered encouragement. Sue said, "It is unquestionably easier to handle your husband's absences when you only have to worry about yourself, but being alone with children gets easier. By the time our oldest two were six and nine, they were company for me, and there wasn't the same stress involved in their care that you have with infants and toddlers."

Other mothers advise, "Don't try to do as much as if you had a husband around." Also, "If you act like this is a normal way to live, your children are more likely to accept that it is."

Finally, mothers home alone need to hang on to this: "The LORD himself goes before you and will be with you; he will never leave you nor forsake you. Do not be afraid; do not be discouraged" (Deuteronomy 31:8).

Suggested Further Reading

Barnes, Robert. *Who's in Charge Here? Overcoming Power Struggle with Your Kids*. Dallas: Word, 1990. The title says it all. Excellent!

Samalin, Nancy with Martha Moraghan Jablow. *Loving Your Child Is Not Enough: Positive Discipline That Works*. New York: Viking, 1987. Affirms value of discipline without being punitive; also helps parents know when they have said enough.

Sprinkle, Patricia H. *Do I Have To? What to Do About Children Who Do Too Little Around the House*. Grand Rapids: Zondervan, 1993. Why children need household responsibilities, how to teach skills instead of chores, age-appropriate skills, and how to build a family team.

CHAPTER SEVENTEEN

When the Children Are Sick

Lord, is my child really sick? He's had a cough for a week, and seems listless. Is it allergies, or something more serious? I don't want to make a foolish, expensive doctor's visit, but neither do I want to be an irresponsible mother. How can I tell if he's sick enough to see a doctor?

One dilemma mothers home alone face frequently is having a sick child, not knowing how sick he or she is, and having no one to consult. Suzanne says, "My son has a habit of getting sick when his daddy's out of town. I don't know whether to take him to the doctor or not. I worry a lot more than I used to."

Not only does the mother home alone have to make all the decisions, she has an additional hassle if she has more than one child. Allison said, "One of my sons has asthma. When he has an attack, I have to call a neighbor to watch the other two children while I take him to the emergency room."

Working moms face a third problem. Teale, who teaches school, says, "When my kids get sick, I'm up a creek, because my job isn't flexible. One son got sick at the school where I teach. I kept him with me the rest of that day, but the next day his fever was

worse. I had to go to school, so I did what I had to: left him home by himself. I was in tears most of the morning. Finally my principal called a substitute so I could take him to the doctor."

According to those with experience, a mom home alone needs:

- A pediatrician she trusts.
- Someone to consult with on medical decisions—a friend, another single mom, or a family member.
- A good pediatric health care manual, kept in easy reach.
- A well-stocked first-aid kit. (*See Checklist 2, back of book.*)

A word of wisdom: stay calm. Your child will take his or her cues from you. If you are frantic, the child will be, too.

SITUATIONS REQUIRING IMMEDIATE EMERGENCY ATTENTION

The *Boy Scout Handbook*, one of the best short emergency medical guides available, lists five situations that *always* need immediate, emergency care:[1]

stopped breathing	needs	rescue breathing
no heartbeat	needs	CPR
severe bleeding	needs	pressure
choking	needs	Heimlich maneuver
poisoning	needs	call poison control center

In none of these situations will you have time to read a book! If you are alone with small children, learn how to perform these maneuvers before you need them!

TIPS FOR MAKING THE TOUGH CALLS

A newspaper interview with several pediatricians gave these guidelines for when to take a child to the emergency room, when you can wait for an office visit, and when you can treat the situation at home.[2] Here is their advice.

When to Call 911

If a child's skin is dusky, or she is gasping or has trouble breathing. An airway may be obstructed.

When to Go to the Emergency Room

For infants, go to the emergency room for

- Any noticeable decrease in urination.
- Bulging or depression of the soft spot.
- Repeated vomiting. A baby gets dehydrated easily.
- Any fever, if the child is younger than three months.

If you have a responsive pediatrician, call for instructions, but if there is any delay, go to a hospital emergency room. Infants are vulnerable to sepsis, a rapidly spreading blood infection that needs immediate treatment.

For toddlers and older children, go to the emergency room for

- Repeated vomiting, strange behavior, or loss of consciousness after a bump to the head.
- Rashes and bug bites that cause swelling around the mouth, difficulty in breathing, or purple, bruise-like rashes—especially accompanied by fever. Can indicate blood infection.
- Stomach pain accompanied by blood in urine or stool.
- Severe stomachache that seems centered in the right lower abdomen. Could be appendicitis, especially if the child also has low-grade fever and nausea.
- Suspected broken bone.
- Signs of a break: protruding bone, deformity, decreased function, diminished color, and white nail beds. A milder injury like a sprain is best evaluated at a doctor's office.

When to Go to the Doctor's Office

Make an immediate appointment with your doctor when the following conditions exist:

- Fever of 104 or higher in toddlers and 102 or higher for a day in school-age children.
- Listlessness even after acetaminophen begins to bring down a fever; stiffness or a pain in the neck; or pain in the head. Can all be symptoms of meningitis or blood infection.

Two toddler conditions better seen at a pediatrician's office than in an emergency room: dislocated elbow, and a bright red sore throat. Emergency rooms may overtreat these conditions, which are simpler and far more common among toddlers than among adults.

A Special Word About Teens

Most teens have few ailments beyond colds, flu, and acne. Persistent headache or stomachache may be the result of stress rather than something serious, but should be evaluated by a doctor. A teen exhibiting signs of drinking or drug use should also be seen by a family physician or a counselor. A teen who cannot stand up, cannot stay awake, or is behaving uncharacteristically should be taken to an emergency room, particularly if you think the teen may have used drugs.

A FINAL WORD: PREVENTION

At the end of Chapter 7, I suggested some home health care manuals a woman home alone can use to check symptoms against. A good manual is particularly important for a mother home alone.

In addition, mothers home alone need to take special precautions to keep their children away from other children with infectious diseases. Teale said, "One thing I've learned: when I'm alone, we don't go out much. It gets everybody off their schedule, and they are more likely to bring home germs. Dealing with sick kids, a job, and an absent father is more than I want to handle."

Just as important, women home alone with children need to keep shots up-to-date. Did you know that up to half of U.S. children do not get all their polio shots?

If you cannot afford to have children vaccinated at a doctor's office, make an appointment with your local health department. Having watched my friend Bonnie, who was attacked by polio in 1950, struggle as she lives alone in a wheelchair, I urge mothers alone not to risk that kind of future for your children when it's preventable!

CHAPTER EIGHTEEN

Families Where Dad Comes and Goes

One father tells this story: "*For several years my job required extensive travel. After every long trip, my wife and four children met me at the door with loving hugs and kisses. During one happy homecoming, I gathered my youngest child in my arms and asked, 'What do you want to be when you grow up?'*

"*Without hesitation she said, 'A pilot.'*

"*'Why?' I asked, surprised.*

"*Gazing at me intently, she replied, 'So I can spend more time with you.'*

"*Shortly thereafter, I accepted a position that required far less travel.*"[1]

A married mom whose husband's work frequently takes him away from the family has two definite advantages over a single mom: a paycheck, and someone who comes home to provide love, support, and relief from single parenting.

The down side, however, is that she must work hard to stabilize a family that swings from sometimes having one parent to sometimes having two. Priscilla, whose ex-husband worked on an oil rig, remembers, "It was sort of like running water. When he was gone I had to be both hot *and* cold, but when he was there I was supposed to be just hot *or* cold."

Absent dads miss Little League games and piano recitals, report cards, class plays, award days, the excitement of losing the first tooth or taking the first step, the sorrow of failing a test or burying the family dog. Their wives get to deal with the children's disappointment and even heartbreak. A doctor's wife said with a sigh, "I never know whether to buy two tickets or one. We don't know when he's going to have to leave on an emergency."

"I don't think we'd have gotten a video camera if my husband didn't fly," a pilot's wife said, "but it's one way of keeping him in touch with what the kids are doing. He's missing so much."

Even when he isn't missing anything special, schedules have to be adapted to his coming and going. "Getting everybody off in the morning is rough when he's gone," says Teale. "I teach, and we all have to leave by seven. When my husband is home, he keeps our three boys going while I dress. Sometimes I don't leave my room until I'm ready. But when he's gone, I have to do it all. I sometimes don't even get my makeup on!"

Moms with frequently absent husbands agree that one of their hardest tasks is helping the family keep in touch. Children get used to taking problems and joys to Mom, which may leave Dad feeling left out. Children get used to obeying Mom, which may anger Dad. And if Dad is away very long at a stretch, he may even be a stranger to very young children.

Sue's husband was shipped out within a week of the birth of each of their three children. She remembers, "When he came home one time, the infant screamed if his daddy tried to pick him up. Then, about the time the baby got used to him, Dad had to leave again."

Here are some suggestions married mothers home alone give to help children and their absent fathers keep in touch:

STAYING IN TOUCH WHILE DAD IS AWAY

1. Prepare children ahead of time. Whether two or sixteen, children like to know what's going on in their families. Talk about the trip and look at a calendar to note when Dad will leave and come back. If an early morning departure is involved, let children know the night before that he will be gone before they wake up.

Lynn's family carefully prepares for her husband's overseas mission trips. "We think our two children need to feel they are a part of their dad's ministry. Before he leaves, we all gather and compare schedules. We talk about what he will miss, and we pray for each person in the family. When he's gone, we know what he's doing each day, and he knows what we'll be doing each day. He also talks over what he's going to miss with each child. 'I'm not happy to be gone while you are having your awards ceremony. How do you feel about that?' We all appreciate that he thinks about us and the implications for us before he commits himself to a trip."

2. Mark the family calendar. Older children appreciate having Dad's departures and predicted arrivals clearly marked. Once children also get involved in activities that sometimes take them away overnight, you might draw a yellow line through days on the family calendar when *any* family member will be away.

Use a visual aid to help young children understand how long Daddy will be away. Some families make a paper chain with a link for each day Daddy will be gone and tear off the links together. Key used pennies in a jar, instead. "You can privately add or take out pennies if his plans change," she confides.

3. Ask Dad to leave something special behind. This is particularly important for small children or long trips. Some fathers leave notes or tiny presents. Lynn's husband made coupons for her to distribute while he was gone, one coupon per day for cooperation. The coupons were good for a pack of gum, a visit to the popcorn shop, or a special treat.

When Karen's husband went to sea, he made tapes for the children to listen to at bedtime. "He read their favorite books and Bible stories, sang their favorite songs, told jokes, or just said how much he missed them. They didn't mind hearing the same tape over and over. They would listen to Daddy for an hour before bed, and I'd get an hour off in another room. I loved hearing his voice, too. It was like having him in the house."

4. Don't always schedule phone calls after the children are in bed. Some fathers call in the early evening just to talk with the children. "My girls love talking to their dad on the phone," Martha says. "They feel so special knowing the call is for them."

5. Take advantage of technology. Allison faxes report cards or special papers to Dad the day they come home from school. And if Dad has a laptop computer, you can exchange daily messages by E-mail.

ADJUSTING TO REENTRY

1. Help children understand that Dad is tired. Reentry is hard on everybody. Children need to be warned that the moment Dad comes home is not the best time to acquaint him with disasters, sorrows, or even tremendous events that happened while he was away. They need to be helped to understand that he may need to slump in a chair for a while because he's exhausted.

2. Expect ambivalent feelings. Dad may come home feeling left out of the family, and act extra tough to assert himself as the head of the household. Key says with a wry grin, "One problem we have when he's been in command of a ship and then comes home, he has trouble remembering we're not his crewmen!"

Mom, too, may have ambivalent feelings. Martha says, "I want him to take over the children right away, but I want to stay in charge of everything else!"

Older children who have settled into a looser routine may resent Dad as an intruder. And young children have their own ambivalence. Lauren says, "When my husband is away and comes home, my little boy won't have anything to do with him at first. He's gotten used to it just being him and me, and Daddy comes home to bust that up. When his dad tries to put him to bed or help him in the bathroom, he screams, 'No! I want Mommy!'"

A shared family meal with leisurely time to talk afterwards can be a relaxed way to get back in touch. Unfortunately, the most likely entry, especially with children in the house, involves dashing off to a sports event, finishing homework, or putting cranky children to bed. Several mothers suggest with a shrug, "You do the best you can and don't expect too much of anybody that first night home."

SHARING DISCIPLINE ON A PART-TIME BASIS

This is probably the hardest part of parenting in a "come and go" family. Children who have one parent some days and two parents other days may not be certain whom they are supposed to obey—or why. When my sons were young, I took a temporary job in which I logged sixty thousand frequent flier miles in two years. One evening when I corrected my seven-year-old's table manners, he replied seriously, "Mama, you aren't home enough anymore to tell us what to do." He wasn't being impudent, he was being honest.

Common Discipline Problems

Both parents are too lenient. Dad doesn't want to be "tough" on the kids when he's home so seldom; Mom doesn't want to look like the "heavy" all the time. As a result, children do not get consistent firmness from either parent.

Different parents have different rules. This confuses children, or creates manipulating little schemers who know which parent to approach to get what they want.

Mother postpones discipline until Dad gets home. This means that punishment seldom occurs soon enough after misbehavior to teach new behavior. Furthermore, Dad's return is anticipated with dread rather than delight.

Each parent blames the other for children's misbehavior. "Why can't you control those kids?"

None of those situations is good for children. Mothers I interviewed agreed that families where Dad's away a lot especially need consistent discipline. Sue says thoughtfully, "We agree on the management of our children, so there's no gap whether he's away or here." Allison agrees. "I may have to make some decisions that don't really thrill him, but he backs me up. That way the kids don't have a problem obeying him when he's home for the weekend."

Parents who are frequently separated and have never agreed on family rules and consistent discipline for their children need to make this a priority issue.

How to Set Rules That Don't Work

Some families have gotten into a laissez-faire pattern of rule-setting: Parent One sees a problem and complains about it. Parent

Two says, "Okay, what do you want to do about it?" and Parent One makes a rule.

What happens then? Parent Two lets the child or children break the rule when Parent One isn't there. "Okay, just this once while Mama is at PTA you can watch television instead of doing your homework" or "Since Dad's out of town, you don't have to mow."

As a result, children know that a rule isn't really a family rule—and learn to play one parent against the other.

Setting Rules That do Work

To break that cycle, the parent who names most problems and makes most rules can back off and ask, "Do *you* see a problem here? What do *you* think we need to do?" Then wait for Parent Two to suggest a solution both parents will enforce.

Another solution is for each parent to write down a suggestion for dealing with a problem and compare them, trying to come to a mutually agreeable solution.

The time that Dad travels can actually help the family deal with family issues like discipline. Parents while apart can study and reflect on an issue without discussions turning into the same old arguments. Some parents choose a book on discipline or family life, read it separately, write down personal reflections about how that book relates to their own family issues, and share those reflections via telephone calls. Thinking about the issue separately and sharing thoughts helps them come to joint decisions about family rules and methods of discipline. (See suggested further reading at the end of Chapter 16.)

Expect challenges to discipline when Dad comes home. No matter how consistent your rules and discipline, children of all ages will test them once Dad comes home. Brenda reports, "When my husband had a job that took him away weekly Monday through Thursday, our son retested the limits every single week! It took a few weeks for us to see the pattern: Michael would test, and my husband would be lenient to make up for his absence. Fortunately, we agreed on what needed to be done once we realized what was happening: we had to set limits and stick with them."

Testing takes on different appearances at different ages. Older children may be defiant, smart-mouthed, even rude. Very young children may cling to their mother for support.

Parents who prepare themselves for reentry problems won't need to feel hurt, rejected, or exasperated at less-than-perfect obedience when Dad returns. Sympathetic firmness rather than tolerance is important, however, and both Mom and Dad need to observe the same limits and teach children that whomever they ask, "No" means "No!"

WHILE DAD'S AWAY, LET THE FAMILY PLAY

While discipline needs to remain firm, other parts of family life can "go casual" while Dad's away. Here are some suggestions:

1. Make eating more fun. Most families slack up on meals while Dad's gone. Some eat informally in front of the television, or have a lot of picnics. Others eat out a lot. "Too much junk food," several mothers admitted ruefully. But there are healthier alternatives, such as cafeterias with wide selections of vegetables or inexpensive restaurants.

When I was a child and my mother went away for a few days, Dad always took us to Chinese restaurants, because Mother didn't like Chinese food. To this day, whenever I eat at a Chinese restaurant it feels like a treat.

2. Have planned fun together. August takes her children to an early movie, or drops the baby off at a sitter and takes the older three skating. "We don't try to do big things, like going to the beach, but we do have fun."

However, she warns, trying to compensate for Dad's absence with too many treats and activities only results in an exhausted mother and cranky children. "Maintain your daily routine," she advises, "and I find it helps me and the kids if we decide what we're going to do at the beginning of the week—set a specific schedule and limits. Then there's nobody whining to do something else later."

ADVANTAGES OF A TRAVELING DAD

While families with often absent dads have unique problems, children in a family where Dad comes and goes also have advantages other children may not have. Allison said, "One thing that's been fun for us as a family is that sometimes we use my husband's work as a place for mini-vacations. We go with him to a city, and while he's working we 'do' the place, then meet him for dinner. And recently his territory has shifted, so he has customers near where my grandmother and cousins live. We stay in far better touch with relatives now that he drops in to see them when he's in town."

June sees another advantage. "My daughter has had an independence and developed a maturity she might not have otherwise. She has learned to take care of herself in some good ways, and to look for alternative solutions to always having parents around to drive her everywhere. If he's not home to pick her up after cheerleading, she takes a city bus. I think that's made her more mature."

She adds, "Also, when my husband is home, he's completely home. On those days, my daughter sees more of him than her friends do their dads."

IN CONCLUSION

Married mothers home alone have to do everything single moms do, and they also have to stabilize the family, help members keep in touch, maintain consistent discipline, and deal with reentry grouchiness. Some even have to reintroduce children to their daddy! Key tells this story:

"Once when my husband was at sea, our toddler kissed each of us and her daddy's picture every night at bedtime. The night after my husband got home, she gave me and her brother a kiss and hug and turned to go to bed.

"'What about Daddy?' I asked.

She went right past her father to get the picture, brought it back, gave it a big kiss, and headed for bed. He was so hurt! He didn't understand that for seven weeks she'd kissed that picture every night. But the story had a happy ending. Suddenly she looked at the picture, looked up at him, shrieked, 'Daddy!' and ran into his arms."

Maintaining a family with one member frequently gone takes composure, courage, and commitment. A sense of humor helps. Good friends are important. And prayer is essential.

PART FOUR

Money Matters!

INTRODUCTION

It's foolish to take out insurance, lock our cars, and put security systems in our houses, then fail to become educated about money matters that can equally endanger our lives and happiness.

Certified financial planner Mary Lynne McDonald declares that women who neglect to become educated about money often find themselves "in really bad financial condition, with limited solutions, little knowledge, and no confidence. They are easy prey for the unscrupulous, and they generally make poor financial decisions that they deeply regret later."[1]

Judge Lois Forer wrote *What Every Woman Needs to Know Before (and After) She Gets Involved with Men & Money*, because of her experience "in sordid courtrooms where I saw the sad results that befell good, decent, intelligent women who had been caught up by legal myths and ideals" and did not know how to protect themselves financially.[2]

While learning about money may seem complicated, unpleasant, and even boring, no woman home alone can afford to ignore the subject. The following chapters deal with basic financial matters any woman needs to know, how to make major purchases with confidence, financial planning for a more reassuring future, financial questions to ask before you marry, and things a married woman home alone especially needs to know.

A WISE WOMAN KNOWS
*Any woman who does not learn
to look after herself financially
is sabotaging herself as surely
as if she set a time bomb under the bed.*[3]

CHAPTER NINETEEN

*B*asic Finances Any Woman Needs to Know

Most of us would far rather read a book than keep one. When Judi was widowed, "Taking over the books was the hardest part. His secretary paid all our bills, and continued to do so for a year after he died. When I took over the books, I didn't know anything."

Jayne had a similar experience after her divorce. "Paying bills was hard for me. My money situation changed dramatically, and I had to handle everything myself."

Keeping books is not hard. It simply involves listing what you spend, what you earn, and subtracting the smaller from the larger to keep a running total. Hopefully, the earnings are larger.

We need to keep books both to stay abreast of how much money we have and to prepare tax forms. Accountants give a few simple tips for keeping your own books:

1. Balancing a checkbook. Balancing a checkbook means making certain that what the bank thinks you have and what you think you have are the same. If you have never balanced a checkbook, go to your bank and ask one of the customer assistants to show you how to use your monthly statement to keep an accurate balance. It's as simple as third-grade math: addition and subtraction. If you have teenagers, take them with you. They need to learn, too.

2. If you want to keep books by hand: Buy a ledger at any office-supply store. Use a simple system with one column for income and one for outgo, or a slightly more complicated system with separate columns for various types of expenses—household, groceries, clothes, contributions, utilities, etc.—so you can see at a glance what you are spending money for.

3. You can buy an easy-to-use computer program to keep your books. These programs (our family uses Quicken) require you to enter each check and its category. Then the program calculates the current balance and prepares an end-of-the-year written report of spending and earnings in various categories. That's particularly helpful for itemizing tax deductions and charitable contributions.

PREPARING TAX FORMS

One reason we keep books is to make it easier to pay taxes. Whether you pay someone else to do your taxes or do them yourself, you will need to assemble receipts, canceled checks, and W–2 forms if you are employed. To make tax time easier

1. Keep receipts in one place. If you itemize (list) deductions, you need receipts or canceled checks for all items you deduct. If you keep all receipts and canceled checks in one large envelope, drawer, or box, you won't forget or have to search for important ones.

2. Get forms at libraries or government offices. Everyone needs a 1040 form, either simple or long. People who own a business or freelance (writers, artists, musicians), own stocks, etc., have to use additional forms. When you pick up your 1040 form, scan the list to see which other forms you need so you don't have to go back. Get an extra copy of each form to use as a worksheet.

3. Use a sample form for your first draft. Assemble a calculator, receipts, and canceled checks, forms, pencil, and pen. Read each section's instructions just before you fill in that section. Pencil in one form so you can erase, then copy on a second form in ink. Mail the second form, with a check if you owe money, to the IRS address in the booklet. The booklet will also tell how to pay taxes by phone, if you prefer.

4. Keep tax forms and receipts for seven years. Save your penciled form and all receipts and checks. The IRS may want to see them.

5. A good attitude makes tax time easier. Paying taxes is one way we render to Caesar what belongs to Caesar. As you pay taxes, think of good things they provide: roads, clean water, orderly government, education for children, care for those who cannot care for themselves. Also remember what has happened to you in the past year. If it was good, thank God for that. If it was awful, thank God it's over!

The early Christians must have grumbled about paying taxes, too, for the apostle Paul wrote to the Romans: "It is necessary to submit to the authorities, not only because of possible punishment but also because of conscience. This is also why you pay taxes, for the authorities are God's servants, who give their full time to governing. . . . if you owe taxes, pay taxes" (Romans 13:5–7).

REMEMBER: Taxes are due April 15.

FINANCIAL RECORDS TO KEEP HANDY

Lauren, who is savvy about financial things, told me, "I keep a book that lists where every account we have is, where our wills are, every insurance policy we have, details about social security numbers, birth certificates, IRAs, stocks, and property deeds. It stays in a locked filing cabinet, and I keep it up-to-date. If anything happened, I could put my hands on any documents I needed."

She sets a good example the rest of us need to follow! *Checklist 4 lists papers to keep handy at home and papers to keep in your safety deposit box.* I personally also carry all family Social Security numbers on a card in my wallet. It's amazing how often I need them.

OVERSEEING YOUR CREDIT RATING

Your "credit rating" is a history of your promptness in paying debts, as reported by your creditors, and whether you have filed for bankruptcy or had a tax lien or judgment recorded against you.

After her divorce, Doreen had trouble getting a credit card from a bank. Baffled, she called a credit bureau and asked to see her credit statement. "It was full of errors. My birthday was wrong. It said I'd lived here three years when I'd lived here twenty-five years—I'd just been divorced for three years. It said I'd been employed at my present job for two years, when it's been eighteen. I discovered that when applying for a home equity loan, the bank considers your upper allowable limit on all credit cards as debt even if you have paid off a card. They add up the maximum you *could* borrow and consider *that* your actual debt. I had one account listed on my statement that I'd never heard of.

"I had also co-signed my grown sons' credit cards, and when they were late in their payments, that went on my record as 'poor payment schedule.' I'd never been late paying a bill in my life! I learned you can fill in a dispute form and request an addendum to your credit rating that says who it is who was actually late."

To get a copy of your credit record: Three bureaus handle credit records in the United States. If you have been turned down for credit in the past year, you can get one free copy. Otherwise, they charge a modest fee. Call the bureau nearest you.

- Equifax, Atlanta, GA, 1–800–685–1111.
- TRW Information Services, Chatsworth, CA, 1–800–392–1122.
- Trans Union Credit Information Company, Springfield, PA, 1–800–462–8054.

You will receive your complete current credit history, a list of companies requesting information on you in the past year, and a form for you to dispute any data with which you disagree.

FACTS YOU SHOULD KNOW ABOUT YOUR CREDIT RATING

Married couples have separate histories and a joint rating. Reports are kept for each spouse with credit and for the marriage itself. You may request all three reports by paying three fees.

Your payment history is supplied by people with whom you have credit now or have had credit in the past.

Payment of old debts in full does not remove a bad credit history. Credit and collection accounts remain on the record for seven years; courthouse records are on file for seven years; Chapters 7 and 11 bankruptcy records are on file for ten years.

A divorce decree does not release you from legal responsibility on joint accounts. Joint debts remain on your personal credit history until you contact each creditor separately and seek their legal binding release of your obligation. Only then will your personal credit history be updated accordingly.

You can get your name taken off of "preapproved" credit card offers through the mail. Write to your credit bureau and send your name, address, Social Security number, phone number, and signature.

Suggested Further Reading

Burkett, Larry. *The Complete Financial Guide for Single Parents.* Wheaton, IL: Victor Books, 1991. Especially designed to help a single parent budget and plan for the future.

Forer, Lois G. *What Every Woman Needs to Know Before (and After) She Gets Involved with Men & Money.* New York: Rawson Associates, 1993. A thoughtful consideration of how the legal process can work for or against women.

McDonald, Mary Lynne. *The Christian's Guide to Money Matters for Women.* Grand Rapids: Zondervan, 1995. Information on financial planning, budgeting, investing, planning for college education, and retirement, written by a woman and geared toward women. Includes a good chapter on "What If the Breadwinner Dies?"

CHAPTER TWENTY

Making Major Purchases with Confidence

Economists are fond of saying that women manage most of the money in this country. Anybody who believes that needs to peer up the towering banks and insurance companies men have built, or visit the male-dominated floor of a major stock exchange. True, many women pay daily bills, but few feel confident to buy stocks, a home, or even a car without advice from a man—a friend, relative, or even a salesman whom they do not know.

Why have we, as a gender, been slower to move into the world of finance than we were to get the vote? Are we persuaded by Scripture that money is dirty? Do we think that helplessness in financial matters makes us more attractive to men? Are we simply brain-lazy, preferring somebody else do the hard work? Or are we afraid of making a grave mistake?

DEVELOPING CONFIDENCE

Teale confessed frankly, "I've made some wrong choices. One of those time sharing deals called, saying I was going to win a trip somewhere. It sounded too good to be true, but they had to know right then. That should have been a major signal to me, but I was naive and gave them our credit card number. It cost us a hundred dollars! When my husband got home, he was really upset.

It turned out the whole company was a scam. It was a real nightmare! I learned a lesson, though. I don't give anybody our credit card number over the phone. I also don't make major purchases if he's away and we haven't discussed it."

What did Teale learn from that transaction that can help other women home alone?

- Don't give a credit card number to someone who calls you.
- Something that sounds "too good to be true" really is.
- Don't trust salespeople who insist they have to have a decision right away.

Unfortunately, she also learned not to make major purchases with confidence. However, we women need to know that most men have also been burned at one time or another, and they too learned from their mistakes.

TO MAKE MAJOR PURCHASES WITH CONFIDENCE

1. Research before you buy. Read *Consumer Reports* or a magazine specializing in evaluating the product you want to buy. See which brands they rate high on performance, price, maintenance, and other features important to you.

Consumer Reports also offers three pricing services for new and used cars and other items. For information, call 1–800–234–1645.

2. Compare. Go to several retailers and compare prices for the item you want. If finances are tight, ask about reconditioned secondhand products. For large items, ask whether there is a charge for delivery. You can get some of this information by phone once you know the brand and model year you want.

3. Negotiate. Once you've found the store you think you want to trade with, negotiate with the salesperson. Ask if there's a discount if the item is scratched or dented or if you are paying cash.

4. Have a confident attitude. As you make the purchase, constantly remind yourself: "I'm an intelligent person. People far less intelligent do this successfully every day. I can do this."

5. Think it over. Go home and think about it for two or three days. If you still feel good about the purchase, go back and sign.

6. Never sign a contract you do not fully understand. Ask for explanations of parts that are confusing.

7. Do NOT let salespersons pressure or intimidate you.
If they try, politely leave and make your purchase somewhere else.

8. When you are done, evaluate your performance. After a good purchase at a good price, congratulate yourself. If you could have done better, consider what you'd do differently next time.

A WISE WOMAN KNOWS
I didn't just make a mistake,
I had a learning experience.

BUYING A CAR

Cars are one of the most expensive items a woman home alone will buy—and the most seductive. It's easy to get carried away by style, color, or a salesman's sea-gray eyes, and forget that the engine is the most important part. Furthermore, cars not only cost more than other items initially, they keep on costing if we get a lemon!

No wonder women are so reluctant to buy a car without a man's advice. But I'll let you in on a secret—how careful men buy a car:

1. Research to determine a fair price. In addition to the *Consumer Reports* buying service, ask at a library reference desk for "The Blue Book of Automobile Values" (which is actually yellow). It comes out quarterly and lists three prices for each make and year of automobile:

- the average price dealers are giving on trade-in,
- the average price it has brought in private sales, and
- the average price dealers are selling it for currently.

2. Set a price range before you look. Because car salespeople exert so much pressure on buyers, decide before you begin to look exactly how much you are willing or able to pay down, the maximum you are willing or able to pay monthly, and for how long.

Three-year loans are usually wiser than five-year ones, because while low payments over five years sound good, you will pay a good bit of interest and the car will depreciate faster than it gets paid off. The buyer who tries to resell it or has a major accident and enters an insurance claim may discover she owes more than she can get for the car!

3. Compare prices and negotiate. Armed with information about what you ought to pay and can afford to pay for a car, shop around. Get the best price you can for what you want. Some credit unions will shop for members and get an excellent deal, for a small fee.

If a dealer starts talking about giving you a higher trade-in than you know your car is worth, be wary. He or she is jacking the price up on the other end.

4. Examine the vehicle. Once you have a car you think you want to buy, don't be misled by curb appeal, plush carpet, or new-car smell. Test-drive it. You are not driving a "type" of car, but this particular one! Drive it both fast and slow. Listen for rattles, squealing brakes, or funny noises.

5. Go home and think it over for two or three days before you commit. To hear the ads, car sales are always the biggest, hottest, and shortest in town. Don't let them convince you the sale will be over if you delay; they—or someone else—will have another.

6. Read any contract carefully and be sure you understand it before you sign.

If Buying a Used Car:

1. Know the blue book price and negotiate toward that. Adjust your offer based on mileage and the condition of the car.

2. If buying from a dealer, insist on a warranty.

3. If buying in a private sale without a warranty, ask permission to take it to a mechanic you trust for a checkup. Ask the mechanic to note any problems the car is likely to have in the near future. Then decide whether to close the deal, pass, or make an offer based on money you may need to spend on repairs. If the seller is reluctant to let you take it to your mechanic, ask him or her to go with you. Do *not* buy a used car from someone who refuses to let you get it checked out. A woman home alone doesn't need problems she's paid for!

SELLING A CAR

1. Set a fair price. It's hard to know how to put a value on something that has faithfully carried us through sleet and rain—or left us stranded on an expressway in rush hour. Your price will partly depend on how badly you need or want to get rid of the car, but you don't need to set it too low. Everybody likes a bargain, so set a price that gives a buyer some room to negotiate—three or four hundred dollars more than you expect to get. To get a sensible price range, take the blue book value and adjust for mileage and condition.

2. Simple repairs may increase the value. Clean the upholstery and carpets, touch up paint, glue parts that are unglued. Your buyer is looking for a good buy!

LEGAL PROCEDURES FOR BUYING OR SELLING A CAR

1. Transfer of title. The "title" is a deed showing who owns the car. A dealer will do this for you. If you buy or sell a car privately, transfer of title must be part of the process. That is a simple matter of the current owner signing the title on the back, indicating that the car has been sold. If you borrow money from a bank to pay for the car, they will hold the title until you make the last payment. *Never* buy a car without a title.

2. Insurance. Once the car is yours, you need insurance. Before you buy a car, get an insurance price estimate. Your existing agent may be able to transfer your old policy. Or consult *Consumer Reports* for ratings of various companies and call several. Once the car is yours, call again to "get a binder" on the coverage you agreed on.

3. Registration and valid tag. Your new car must be registered in your state. A dealer will do that for you. If buying from an individual, look in the blue pages of the phone book and call the state Division of Highway Safety and Motor Vehicles to find out what your state requires. If you bought the car in a private deal, you will have to pay sales tax when you register it. In some states you can transfer a tag, others require you to get a new tag.

When the state sends you a notice of registration, if there was any misrepresentation about previous ownership, mileage, and so forth, you can return the car for a full refund.

BUYING A HOME

Not every woman home alone will buy or sell a house, but many do. Two excellent books to walk you through the process are listed at the end of this chapter.

Basic Questions to Ask Before You Buy

1. Can I really do this? Yes! But feel free to ask for help. Read at least one book to learn terms you need to deal with realtors and banks, and don't be afraid to ask people who've recently bought a house for an opinion in a transaction this big. When Sarah Gay tired of paying rent and decided to buy a house, she talked it over with friends, family, even people in her school lunchroom. "I felt I needed input from others in order to make a wise decision."

2. What kind of house do I want? List what you want to do in your house, what spaces you need, and what your neighborhood requirements are. The more clearly you know what you are looking for, the more certain you will be when you find it.

3. What can I afford? Up front you will need a down payment. A standard down payment is twenty percent of the purchase price, but down payments can be much lower for first-time buyers. In addition, up front you will have to pay "points." A point is one percent of the purchase price, paid to the lending institution.

Afterwards, you will have monthly payments. How much can you afford to pay each month? A good rule of thumb: *a monthly payment should be no more than one-fourth of your monthly income.* Couples do well to limit themselves to one-fourth of one income, in case either of them stops working.

Remember, a mortgage has to be paid even if you are temporarily out of work or disabled. Don't be dazzled by paperwork showing you could "afford" a larger house. Realtors and bankers make more money by selling big houses, but if you can't pay, they don't suffer—you do.

4. Should I use a realtor? Buying a house through a realtor is always safer, for they are required to provide you with accurate information about the age, size, and condition of the house and may provide a warranty on appliances, heating units, and plumbing. Furthermore, a realtor knows how to walk you through the legal maze to get a loan and close the deal.

If you don't use a realtor, get a real estate attorney to handle paperwork.

5. *How do I choose a realtor?* A realtor should give you respect. Choose one who listens to what you say about the kind of house, neighborhood, and price range you want. Interview several realtors and get referrals from friends who have recently bought houses or from signs on houses you like. Switch realtors if one tries to bully, intimidate, or patronize you.

Once You Think you Like a House

1. *Use Checklist 8 (page 242) to give the house a thorough going-over.*

2. *Make your offer.* The realtor will walk you through the actual purchase. You, however, will need to decide on the price you are willing to pay. To determine your offer:

3. *Use a professional building inspector to make sure the house is in good condition.* Make the sale contingent on your satisfaction with the inspector's report.

4. *Compare the asking price with other sales in that neighborhood.* Ask your agent what comparable houses in the same neighborhood have sold for in the past year. The city assessor's office can tell you how much the seller paid for it, how long he or she has owned it, and what improvements have been made.

5. *Weigh how well the house meets your needs.* If it's your dream house and you don't want to lose it, offer close to the selling price. If not, consider the market in your target area. If there are many houses for sale, offer less than the asking price. Discuss your offer with your realtor.

How to Close the Deal

When you make an offer, you will be expected to put down "earnest money"—between two and five percent of the purchase price. If your offer is refused, you get the money back. If accepted, it is applied toward the down payment.

A realtor, will walk you through closing. If you buy directly from an owner, you will each need an attorney. Call the local bar association for a referral to an attorney who handles real estate transactions. The paperwork will seem to go on forever, but each piece of it is important.

Insist on title insurance! We once bought a house built on two lots, and through an error in recording the deed, only the deed on the smaller of the two lots was recorded. Nobody discovered the error for two years, but when we did, the title company bore the costs of refiling to rectify the error.

SELLING A HOUSE

In my experience, married women home alone are more likely to have to sell a house than to buy one. Several women I interviewed spoke of times when a husband moved early, leaving them to sell their home. To sell quickly, they advised that you look at your house as a buyer will.

1. Does it have "curb appeal"? They have to come in before they'll buy! Trim bushes, edge lawns, sweep porches, paint peeling shutters, and put out blooming plants. I'm told and believe it: A house always sells faster with blooming flowers in the yard.

2. Does it look "ready to move into"? You do not have to keep a house spotless to sell it. Prospective buyers are looking at the architecture and the things you are leaving behind, not the clutter you plan to take with you. But inside, pay attention to small details. Repair torn screens, loose doorknobs, running toilets, leaky faucets. Wash windows. Make sure the doorbell rings. Replace burned-out lightbulbs. Freshen up dirty wallpaper and touch up paint. Wash curtains and blinds.

Straighten basements, garages, and closets so buyers can see how much space there is. Arrange furniture to show how large rooms are. Shampoo rugs. Use good-smelling cleaners or bake often so the house smells good. If you have pets, board them out while you are selling the house. If the pets have left an odor (you may not smell it, so ask a friend), get rid of it!

Realtor or For Sale by Owner?

When you have your house in shape to sell, you have to decide whether to call a realtor or sell it yourself.

Good reasons to use a realtor include:

- Buyers are screened to exclude mere lookers and those who won't qualify for a loan.
- Contracts are carefully written to protect the seller and the buyer.
- You don't have to be nervous about showing strangers through your house.
- You don't have the hassle of arranging the closing.
- The realtor will do the paperwork and help the buyer arrange financing.

1. How to choose a realtor. Do not select a realtor because he or she is a friend! Interview three or four. Tell them up front you are interviewing several, and ask them to come look at your house. Ask what price they would suggest. Also ask what they feel you need to do to the house to make it more saleable. Choose the one whose answers and personality you are most comfortable with.

2. For sale by owner. This route, of course, avoids a realtor's commission, but you must:

- Stay home and be willing to show the house yourself.
- Have someone nearby to call in case of trouble.
- Be comfortable working with a lawyer on closing and contracts.
- Enjoy selling.
- Have no deadline for the sale.

Tips for Selling a House Yourself

1. Learn from others' experience. Talk with friends who have sold houses, or read books and magazine articles on the subject.

2. Get the house ready to move into. (Described above.) Concentrate especially on curb appeal, to entice people inside.

Buy a large sign. Hardware and builder supply stores sell signs and stick-on letters and numbers, which look more professional than hand lettering. Buy a sign you can read from both sides and place it prominently in your front yard. Put your phone number and the number of bedrooms/bathrooms on the sign. If you really want to sell, be prepared to show the house to people who knock on the door.

If your community prohibits signs, seek other creative ways to advertise: notices on public bulletin boards, fliers in neighbors' mailboxes, ads in the newspaper, and weekly advertising flyers.

3. Write a catchy ad. Don't waste words describing what's ordinary; use your word limit to highlight what you like best about your home. If the house is particularly attractive from the street, you may include the address. Try to attract people like yourself, who will appreciate the same unique features you do about your home.

4. Print up an information sheet. Hand it out to friends, coworkers, and at the door to prospective buyers. Include address, square footage, rooms, type of heat, schools, convenient stores, average utility costs, property taxes, appliances to stay (with dates if known), special features of the house and yard, and your asking price.

5. Stay home. Arrange to have someone with you if you are nervous. Put away any valuables. When prospective buyers come, walk through with them to point out special features, then drop back and let them look. Steel yourself for a few rude remarks.

6. Find a lawyer specializing in real estate transactions to help you close the deal. Ask your local bar association to recommend someone.

7. Make sure title insurance is part of the deal.

Suggested Further Reading

Barnes, Kathy, editor. *Better Homes and Gardens' Home Buyer's Guide.* Des Moines: Special Interest Publications, Inc. An annual publication with exceptionally fine articles covering every aspect of home buying.

Sutton, Remar. *Don't Get Taken Everytime: The Insider's Guide to Buying or Leasing Your Next Car or Truck.* New York: Viking Penguin, 1986. Written by a former used car salesman, this book is excellent.

Vila, Bob, with Carl Oglesby, with research by Nena Groskind. *Bob Vila's Guide to Buying Your Dream House.* New York: Little, Brown and Company, 1990. Detailed and quite good.

CHAPTER TWENTY-ONE

𝒫lanning for the Future

Did you know that . . .

- While most women cannot receive Social Security until they are sixty-two unless they are disabled, a widow can begin receiving widow's benefits at sixty?
- An unmarried divorced woman can receive Social Security benefits on her ex-husband's Social Security record if they were married at least ten years and have been divorced two years or more? (Benefits start at sixty-two, and the two-year waiting period is waived if he was receiving Social Security benefits before the divorce.)
- Many divorced women get a higher benefit based on their ex-husband's work record than they get on their own record, especially after he dies?
- You must fill out a name change form with Social Security if you change your name in order for your benefits to be applied to the correct account?
- If you do not audit your Social Security account (or your husband's) every three years and it contains an error—such as no record of earnings and hence no accrued benefits—you cannot change or correct errors more than three years back?

Social Security pamphlets to inform women about the program, their rights, and probable benefits are listed at the end of this chapter.

FINANCIAL PLANNING

Jayne expressed the fears of many women home alone: "I worry about whether there will be enough for my old age."

A financial plan is one way to get rid of excessive debt, develop better spending patterns, and set goals for a reassuring future. Yet many women who are skillful at keeping books, assertive about buying a house, and able to simultaneously hold down a complicated job and run a household avoid sitting down and making a financial plan. Why? Because it looks so complicated. It isn't.

Financial planning begins with a simple equation:

$$\begin{array}{r} \text{TOTAL ASSETS (what you own)} \\ -\ \text{LIABILITIES (what you owe)} \\ \hline \text{NET WORTH} \end{array}$$

Assets are the combined value of anything that can be sold to raise cash: house, cars, jewelry, cash value of insurance, stocks, CDs, mutual funds, bank accounts, IRA or pension plans, collectibles.

Liabilities are debts: balance owed on a mortgage or on credit cards, student loan balances, car or home improvement loans, bank or credit union loans, and personal loans.

When you work it all out, you may be surprised to find you are worth more than you thought!

CHARACTERISTICS OF A GOOD FINANCIAL PLAN

1. A good financial plan makes certain that net worth assets are protected by adequate insurance.

2. A clear financial plan defines financial goals and outlines a realistic plan to achieve them. Each of us dreams about things we'd love to have. We also know there are things we will need. A financial plan helps us save for what we need with some left over to fulfill our dreams. A good financial plan involves three types of goals:

- *Short-term immediate goals:* such as buying a car or new furniture, putting on a new roof, and establishing and maintaining an adequate emergency fund.
- *Intermediate goals:* expenses that require more savings, such as college tuition or the down payment on a home.
- *Long-term goals:* such as adequate retirement funds or caring for loved ones after death.

3. A sensible financial plan takes into account special situations that come from being a woman. Women earn an average of seventy-two cents to each dollar earned by men in similar jobs. Men seldom leave good salaries to stay home with small children or an aging parent. After a divorce, men's income on the average increases by 42 percent, women's decreases by 74 percent. In charting her financial plan, a woman must take into account those years when she will be earning well and can increase savings and investments, and years when she may not have anything to save at all. As she anticipates upcoming seasons, she can plan her saving/spending patterns accordingly.

4. If you want to begin or expand your own financial plan: read one of the books recommended at the end of this chapter or consult a financial planner in your community.

"To be assured that a financial planner is qualified," Mary Lynn McDonald, author of *The Christian Guide to Money Matters for Women*, advised in a phone interview, "he or she should be certified. The most widely recognized credentials are CFP (Certified Financial Planner) and ChFC (Chartered Financial Consultant)."

SQUEEZING SAVINGS FROM A LIMITED BUDGET

Some financial planners recommend an emergency fund equal to three- to six-months' living expenses. Women home alone may laugh at that, for they are used to accomplishing a surprising amount with very little. "The new challenge is to try to keep our retirement nest egg from being squeezed out by the college costs of our children and the long-term care of our aging parents," writes Claire McIntosh.[1]

Yet most women home alone would like to save something toward the future. How can a woman save when living takes all she has?

Take a Hard Look at Your Current Budget

Everybody has a budget, whether it is written down or not. A budget includes:

- *Fixed expenses:* predictable bills like mortgage or rent, car payments, loan payments, day care, insurance, utilities.
- *Necessities:* things like food and clothing, which can be shaved here and there, but have to be bought.
- *Discretionary expenses:* recreation, extra telephone services, cellular phones, fast-food meals, impulse shopping items, vacations, health clubs, and so on.

How much do you spend in each category in a month? In a year? Check stubs, receipts, and credit card bills can help you find out. If fixed expenses and necessities are nearly as great as total income, it is time to seek higher-paying work or ways to reduce expenses.

1. Reduce predictable bills. Share or find less expensive housing, use less heating/cooling, or find less expensive transportation such as a car pool.

If day care is eating up an enormous part of your budget, is there some expertise or skill you could barter for reduced fees? What about job sharing, or working at home with reduced day care fees?

2. Reduce, then eliminate credit card debt. While credit card balance payment may be a fixed expense, purchases are frequently discretionary items. Credit card interest is high, so most budgets can be vastly improved by putting credit cards in a drawer and paying off the debt.

To make debt payment easier on your budget, consolidate debt into one monthly payment. Most communities have consumer credit counseling agencies that can help, for little or no fee.

3. Monitor discretionary purchases. For three months, track every single purchase of soft drinks, candy bars, video rentals, fast-food meals, and so forth. You may find that your discretionary spending is out of control, and an allowance is in order. How much can you afford to spend on items you actually could live without, items like call waiting, cellular phones, cable television, newspapers, magazines, health club memberships, computer networks, junk food, and impulsive shopping items? Limit yourself accordingly.

4. Put savings on the "fixed" income side of the ledger. Usually savings and investment are considered discretionary items. In other words, we put into savings "what we have left." But who ever has anything left? One budget strategy, therefore, is to move savings to the fixed income category, by paying your savings each month as you pay regular bills. Or have savings dollars automatically deposited from your paycheck before you see them.

5. Save what you used to spend. Once you pay off a loan, funnel the amount you used to pay on the debt each month into savings. Do the same with a raise or bonus.

BECOMING AN INVESTOR

"The transition from spender to saver to investor takes discipline, but the rewards are worth it. You'll be the captain of your financial ship with your bills paid, your goals met, and your family protected. Peace of mind may be the most priceless treasure of all."[2]

Doesn't that sound wonderful?

A girl in my college class told this story: After World War II, her mother had a bit of money, so she decided to buy stocks. She reasoned that soldiers coming home would want to fix up their houses, so she bought power tool stock. She figured they'd all want to have a good time, so she bought stock in a company that made athletic equipment. And she figured that people were going to want to move into the future, so she bought stock in a brand-new field, IBM computers. My friend was three years old when her mother bought stock. It sent her to college.

On the other hand, most of us, like Penelope Russianoff, have "heard tale of widows who had no knowledge of money management being robbed blind by CPAs or 'investment counselors' who were either inept or corrupt."[3] How can a woman home alone know whether to invest and how to invest wisely?

1. Find an expert you can trust. Just because your brother-in-law or best friend's husband dabbles in the stock market, you don't necessarily want them to do your investing for you. You need to find someone to advise you who knows different markets well and who has a proven track record of handling other people's money. Mary Lynn McDonald, whose book contains much helpful information for women on investing, said in her interview, "The most objective advice will come from a 'fee-only' planner, who won't try to sell you a product."

Another helpful resource on financial planning is Gary D. Moore's A *Thoughtful Christian's Guide to Investing*, which also offers a newsletter. Moore advises, "If possible, you need to know a broker's heart and capabilities. Referral is the best way to do this. Ask someone you trust, perhaps your minister or a church board member or an accountant."[4]

2. Remember, this is business. Moore also cautions, "Widows are often sentimental about investments that were made by their husbands. For example, a widow may need dependable, tax-free income, but because she remembers how much her mate enjoyed playing the stock market, she'll keep his stocks. You should never, ever be sentimental about investments."[5]

Similarly, you should never be sentimental about your financial advisor or stockbroker! If, after a couple of years with them, they have not increased your investments, change! If you cannot choose between two, give each a small amount to invest and evaluate their track record after a year. If one seems to have a better grasp of what works for your situation, go with that one.

3. Start small. If you are a new investor, consider starting small by investing monthly in a mutual fund. This can provide monthly discipline and safety because of diversification, and it can even result in a higher long-term yield than individual stocks.

If you want to purchase stocks, begin by putting a few dollars in a company that you often use and that gives you good service, good prices, and good products.

4. Get informed. Read books such as those suggested at the end of this chapter. You may even want to take an investment seminar or local college course.

IN CONCLUSION

"Ultimately," Gary Moore insists, "YOU are responsible for your own financial affairs. You may need professional advice at some point, but you also need a basic understanding of what is involved to ensure that the relationship is of mutual benefit."[6]

Lynn Caine, from the anguish of widowhood, cries, "Why should any woman face deprivation and anxiety and financial terror because her husband dies?"[7]

Why should *any* woman face deprivation, anxiety, or financial terror because she fails to take responsibility for her own financial situation? Women home alone need to inform themselves about financial matters to protect themselves, their children, and their retirement years. Good stewardship of what we have been given demands no less.

Suggested Further Reading

Broussard, Cheryl. *The Black Woman's Guide to Financial Independence*. Oakland, CA: Hyde Park Publishers, 1991. Good investment advice for any woman home alone.

McDonald, Mary Lynne. *The Christian Guide to Money Matters for Women*. Grand Rapids: Zondervan, 1995.

Moore, Gary D. *The Thoughtful Christian's Guide to Investing*. Grand Rapids: Zondervan, 1990. Wisdom on making one's investments count for good in the world rather than merely increasing mighty empires.

Social Security . . . What Every Woman Should Know. U.S. Department of Health and Human Services, publication # 05–10127. To order, call 1–800–772–1213. Also, *Request for a Personal and Benefit Estimate Statement* to help you learn what benefits you are likely to receive upon retirement.

CHAPTER TWENTY-TWO

*M*oney Questions to Ask Before You Marry

This very short chapter is directed at unmarried women home alone who are considering getting married.

While it doesn't sound very romantic, before you tie that knot, be sure your joint financial picture is clear. The very process of discussing joint finances may tell you a good deal about one another. You do know that married couples fight more about money than anything else, don't you?

Shelby White writes, "How you handle money and make financial decisions may be one of the important decisions you make in your marriage. A willingness to share financially is really a part of the mutual trust that underlies a good marriage."[1]

Writing from a more painful position—the judge's bench in a divorce court—Lois Forer advises, "Let the daylight of common sense obtrude upon the moonbeams of romance."[2]

You need, of course, to know everything in this entire section on finances. But you should pay special attention to five additional things *before* you get married:

1. Examine any debt either of you is bringing into the marriage. This is especially important in community property states, where you can be held responsible for each other's previous debts. Even if you are not legally responsible, discovering your new spouse is deeply in debt can sour the sweetest of new marriages. A woman at a conference on women and stress, who asked to remain nameless, told the following story:

"I had two children and was barely scraping by financially before I met my second husband, but I did own my home and a decent car. When I met him, he had a wonderful car, a nice apartment, and several rental properties as well. He took me and the children skiing at his time-share condominium in the Rockies and for a week to his time-share apartment on a Caribbean island. He was good to my children, and I really loved him. I still do.

"He said that after we got married, he just wanted me to stay home and make a home for all of us. However, after the wedding, I discovered that all his property was heavily mortgaged. Even his car was leased. Not long after the wedding, three of his tenants moved out. But the mortgages still had to be paid. He tried to sell some property, but it didn't sell. Then he confessed he also owed the IRS thousands of dollars in back taxes. We wound up selling my car, buying an older one, and taking out a mortgage on my house. And instead of being a homemaker, I'm still working ten years after we got married, trying to pay off his debts and hold the IRS at bay."

2. Check both your credit ratings. This is not so much to make certain you are being aboveboard with one another, although that is important, as to discover if there are errors in either rating before you try to establish a joint one. (See pages 147–149.)

3. Decide whether or not you want to pool all assets. Young couples may not have many assets to pool beyond tennis rackets, cars, and stereo systems, but if you have accumulated savings, investments, and/or property through wise investment, inheritance, or divorce settlements, you need to decide what to put in both names and what to retain in the current owner's name—especially if one of you has children from a previous marriage or someone to whom you wish to leave part of your personal assets. Retain those assets in your own name—and make a new will.

4. *Decide who will pay for what*. While many couples just put all earnings into joint accounts, not everyone does. Some couples have a joint account for major bills and individual accounts for "mad money" and personal expenses. Others divide bills into "he pays" and "she pays." Over the years, as you increase your income, you may even try several ways of handling family finances to find one that works best for you.

Before you marry, talk about this to be sure you *can* talk about it without one or the other assuming he or she makes decisions unilaterally. Just as I was writing this chapter, I read a newspaper article about a woman who was married to a "very sweet man" who, after the wedding, informed her that since they were living in her apartment and she was making good money, she should continue to pay all the living expenses as she had before they got married. That woman should have talked money before she went down the aisle!

5. *Make sure each of you has some money for personal expenses and "fun."* That saves many hassles later over purchases you didn't agree on, and gives you something to buy presents for each other with.

6. *Even if one of you makes all the money, that one should not necessarily make all the financial decisions*. Presumably, if one of you plans to stay home, that is a joint decision. Staying home to care for a house and family is a valuable contribution to the whole family, just as earning wages is. Financial decisions, therefore, should be joint.

A WISE WOMAN KNOWS
Never sign a contract you don't understand.
Especially not a marriage contract.

CHAPTER TWENTY-THREE

What a Wife Home Alone ALSO Needs to Know About Money

"I used to wake up with my teeth clenched thinking, 'You selfish [man]! You didn't leave us enough to provide for our future. And now we're all alone. No husband. No father. No money.' Money! How could I be so bound up in money? . . . What mercenary devil had taken charge of my soul? No devil at all. I have come to recognize that money is important. Women should know more about it." [1]

While married women home alone capably learn to cope with other facets of solitary living, most of the ones I interviewed still leave major financial decisions to their husband. Teale spoke for many when she said, "While my husband is away, I don't make big purchases. I try to wait until he gets back. Once I did buy a mattress on sale, because we'd already planned our budget to buy a mattress, but if we haven't talked about it, I don't do it. And since he has an accounting degree, it makes no sense for me to keep our books. I learned to balance a checkbook and take care of things with the bank, and I pay bills when he's away, but usually he deals with all that."

There are, however, three good reasons a wife home alone needs to know as much as she can about her family's finances: death, divorce, and disaster.

If you aren't ready to think about any of those, consider the following facts:

Facts a Married Woman Needs to Know

- Fifty percent of all women over sixty-five in the U.S. are widows and will remain widows for fifteen years after their husbands die.[2]
- In 1990 there were 11.5 million widows between the ages of thirty and seventy. Half of them were fifty-six or younger.[2]
- One-third of all widows in 1985 were under fifty when their husbands died.[2]
- When a woman divorces, her income on the average drops by 74 percent; his income increases by 42 percent.[3]
- More than 50 percent of divorced men still do not pay full child support.
- Because child support stops at eighteen and many states do not require either parent to contribute toward a child's college education, a single mother may be left with all college bills.
- A valid will must have two witnesses. Some people think that all they have to do to make a will is to type one up, sign it, date it, and put it in a safety deposit box. Only too late do they discover it is invalid.
- A wife is legally responsible for any tax returns she signs. A divorced wife can be financially responsible for any money her ex-husband owed the IRS during their marriage even if the divorce decree states that the husband alone is responsible!

Let's put some personality into those statistics. A missionary went on a routine trip to another country. Five days later, in a foreign city, he dropped dead of a heart attack. His wife was forty-six.

"You just never imagine that could happen," she told me later. "You have to rethink your whole life."

A woman physician, married to a dentist, let him pay all their bills and make major investment decisions. When their marriage ended after nine years, she discovered he had paid his dental school bills and deferred payment on her medical school bills. She entered life as a single mother with thousands of dollars of debt.

When a schoolteacher's husband abandoned her and left the country, she learned that for years he had deferred taxes, reported business expenses he didn't have, and concealed income he did have. In the midst of her grief at his abandonment, she owed eleven thousand dollars in back taxes because she had co-signed their joint tax forms without reading them! She might have been able to claim the "innocent spouse rule" of the IRS and sue him for fraud—but he had disappeared.

Those are all friends of mine. Don't you have friends with similar stories?

MAGICAL THINKING

"That wouldn't happen to me," you object. "My husband is healthy, honest, and faithful, and we have a good marriage."

Several years ago at a brunch with friends, I remarked that if Bob died young, I thought I'd find an isolated beach house where I could live and write.

One of the women shuddered. "How gruesome to be thinking what you'd do without your husband!"

"You ought to *all* think like that," replied another woman who had been unusually quiet that morning. "Where you'd go, how you'd earn a living. Last night my husband told me he wants a divorce. In twenty-three years of marriage I've never imagined life without him. Now I don't know where to begin."

Even wives who will never be divorced need to realize that their lives can change in an instant. One woman I interviewed for this book, a wife in her early forties, spent the night with us several months later. She was on her way to a nearby hospital because her husband, a traveler also in his early forties, had a stroke while on the road. He has recovered, thank God. But if your husband were disabled and you did not understand your family's financial picture, what would happen to you? What would happen to *him?*

To take no interest in finances that impinge on our lives is magical thinking. We blithely assume that even if we are irresponsible, somehow everything will still be all right. We need to read again Matthew 25:1–13, Jesus' own teaching about what happens to women who fail to think seriously about their future.

Ruth Tucker, author of *Multiple Choices: Making Wise Decisions in a Complicated World*, says, "Women need to see themselves as independent and complete without a man. This is as true for women in a good marriage as it is for single women. They need to have access to money and a means of support."[4]

TEN QUESTIONS A WIFE NEEDS TO ASK

Below are some questions any married woman needs to ask—particularly any woman with a husband who frequently travels, has a hazardous occupation, or suffers a chronic disease.

1. *How much do we earn?*
2. *How much are we spending on housing?* Mortgage or rent, utilities, insurance, taxes.
3. *What are our financial assets?* Where are the deeds, titles, or related paperwork for those assets? Assets include real estate, stocks, bonds, cars, boats, valuable collectibles, and anything else that could be sold to provide cash.
4. *How much insurance do we have?* What kind? Where are the policies? How much are the premiums? When are they paid?
5. *What pension plans do we have?* How much will they provide us? What will they provide a surviving spouse? What age do we have to be to begin drawing on them? Where is the paperwork?

Federal laws mandate that wives have a right to share in a husband's pension even if they did not work to earn the funds. However, many plans—including the military—cut benefits significantly if the primary beneficiary dies. (Also see the section on Social Security in Chapter 21.)

6. *What are the provisions of our wills?* Everybody has a will. Either you write it, or the state writes it. But if the state writes it, be assured that the state will benefit. Mary Lynne McDonald advises that each spouse draw up a personal will. "In most cases," she declares, "joint wills do not work." If you have not written wills, when will you draw them up? Please, do it soon.

7. *Do we live in a common law or common property state? Are all assets in both our names?* Your state determines property rights for surviving spouses. If you live in a common law state, you don't automatically own half the property you buy with your husband, even if you pay for it! You have to specify a type of joint tenancy (ownership) when you buy it:

   - *Joint tenancy with right of survivorship.* Any two people who buy property together own the property jointly, and if one dies, the property goes to the other.

   - *Joint tenancy by the entirety.* Same as above, except you must be married to qualify.

   - *Joint tenancy in common.* You each own half the property and can leave your half in whatever way you choose. This is particularly important when partners have separate beneficiaries, such as children from a former marriage.

8. *How much debt do we owe? To whom?* Debt includes a mortgage, credit card balances, home equity loans, college tuition loans, automobile loans, and anything else you still have to pay if one of you dies.

9. *Where is the paperwork on those debts?* Knowing about debt your husband has contracted is important. In some states your personal credit rating is affected by his debts. In a common property state, not knowing about a debt incurred by your spouse will not excuse you from repayment; either spouse is liable for the other's debts in case of death, divorce, or default.

10. *Do I have credit in my own name?* A wife needs to establish her own credit before losing a spouse; otherwise, she may be denied a mortgage, credit card, or other loan.

Allison knows the value of having her own credit[ ]
my parents got divorced, my mother had no credit. I make [ ]
name is on everything now. Otherwise, with my husband tra[ ]
all the time, something could happen to him and I'd have no cr[ ]

A GOOD TIP

Allison also discovered something that may help you, too[ ]
"While I pay all our bills, if he got paid while he was out of town, it[ ]
used to screw me up. I waited for him to come home, get to his
office, and get his check. Some people have automatic deposit, but
we didn't want that. I learned recently that a wife can pick up her
husband's paycheck, sign it with her husband's name, and deposit it
into their joint account. You can't get money back at that transaction, but at least you can deposit money and write checks."

HOW TO TALK ABOUT MONEY WITHOUT A FIGHT

We could postpone talking about money indefinitely if the
stakes weren't so high. In our culture, it's less intimate to talk about
sex! It's also more romantic. But while it's hard to imagine strolling
up to our husband and saying, "Honey, can we talk about what happens if you die or walk out?" one quote I used in the last chapter
bears repeating here: "How you handle money and make financial
decisions may be one of the important decisions you make in your
marriage. A willingness to share financially is really a part of the
mutual trust that underlies a good marriage."[5] That is doubly true
for a family where the woman is often home alone.

Wise couples with a husband who comes and goes need to
set aside a day together to consider: "If either of us died in the next
twelve months, how much would the other have to live on?"
Remember that if a stay-at-home mother dies and leaves small
children, the family will need a housekeeper/sitter.

Make the day as cozy as possible. Resolve not to fight. The
purpose of this day is to gather information, not make permanent
decisions. Get out all the files and tax returns you need. Be sure you
understand terms of the mortgage, car loans, and investments.

You may want to set aside another time to discuss investments jointly. Or you might take a class on investing together at a local community college.

In some marriages, unfortunately, money is equated with power and control. One or both partners think that the person who earns more has the "right" to make decisions about money. The earner may even resist attempts to "pry" into his or her handling of family finances.

If your husband resists talking about money because he earns it all, point out that sharing the information with you is a way of showing love both for you and for the family. My mother-in-law has said several times how much she appreciated her husband taking the trouble to teach her about their finances before his death.

Also point out that you need family financial information not only in case of his death, but in case he is seriously disabled and you need both knowledge and authority to make financial decisions to help take care of him.

If talking about money leads to old familiar quarrels, consider seeking financial counseling.

Meanwhile, a wife needs to know about family finances. Every year the papers list bank accounts nobody has claimed. How many of those belong to widows who never knew that account existed?

If your husband truly won't discuss money, read the family financial files. Read the mail: bank statements, investment account statements, insurance statements, credit card bills. Learn where the money is, how much there is, and where it is kept. Make your own list of bank accounts, credit card accounts, insurance policy numbers. You need to know!

A WARNING ABOUT JOINT TAX RETURNS

In most families husbands do the taxes—not because they want to keep things from their wives, but because the wives don't want to do them. Yet I have mentioned twice already the importance of knowing what is on your tax returns before you sign them. Read your tax returns. And ask questions! Don't worry about sounding ignorant. How else will you learn? What if by this time next year he is disabled, and you have to do taxes alone?

There are three other reasons you should read your tax return:

- You may discover your husband has less income than you thought.
- You may discover he has *more* income than you thought!
- You may discover that your husband is cheating the government, and because you are signing the returns, you could be in trouble.[6]

Never sign a tax return you don't understand or are not willing to uphold in a court of law!

"DIVORCE INSURANCE"

None of us likes to prepare for divorce, particularly if we are in a good marriage. However, whereas divorce used to be a complicated, drawn-out process involving two people who agreed to sever a marriage, a modern no-fault divorce can be obtained by one partner without the other partner's consent. I will never forget the shocked wail of a friend when served with unexpected papers: "I don't even believe in divorce!"

While divorce can be obtained by one party, however, a financial settlement cannot. And divorce lawyers and financial planners report that homemakers and career women are equally naive when it comes to financially protecting themselves in divorce settlements. Too often a wife discovers that "their" accountant has become his accountant, and "their" lawyer his lawyer. At that point, getting a true financial picture can prove to be a nightmare.

To help women caught in divorce settlement proceedings avoid that nightmare, Mary Lynne McDonald, a certified financial planner, has become a "divorce consultant" who analyzes the financial part of a divorce with spreadsheets and graphs. She then testifies in court to work toward a "fair" settlement for both partners. In a free informative handout, "Divorce Isn't Easy . . . But It Can Be Fair," she explains:

> What may look fair today turns out to be less than equitable over time. In a typical marriage the wife generally takes time off to raise children and sacrifices her chances to build her earning

power and contribute to a pension. Her income is often "extra" and the family gears its standard of living to the higher salary of the husband. Both the husband and the wife invest their time and energy in developing the husband's career. In the event of a divorce, the woman is left with the loss of her standard of living and a limited ability to earn a living and build a retirement nest egg. She also loses all the years invested in her husband's career.

Most divorcing couples think 50/50 is a fair asset split because they fail to realize that the earning power is, in fact, an intangible asset. That's why one year after a typical divorce, the standard of living for women with minor children has dropped while the man's has risen.

That's why all wives need what Ruth Tucker calls "Divorce Insurance": "an attitude of partnership in money and family business matters, so that in the event of death or divorce a wife is informed, up-to-date, and prepared and able to make decisions on her own."[7]

THE BOTTOM LINE

Our society likes to talk about "the bottom line" in many things: relationships, projects, commitments. It's a term, of course, taken from accounting, and is particularly relevant here.

The bottom line for a wife home alone is that she needs to know what the family financial situation is, where financial papers are, and how to make financial decisions.

Suggested Further Reading

McDonald, Mary Lynne, CFP. "Divorce Isn't Easy . . . But It Can Be Fair." Pacific Northwest Financial Group, Inc. One-page handout offering help in reaching an equitable divorce settlement. Available by phone or fax: 206–858–8102.

White, Shelby. *What Every Woman Should Know About Her Husband's Money.* New York: Turtle Bay Books, 1992. Frank analysis of how women get into trouble by not knowing about their husbands' money, and suggestions for avoiding common mistakes.

PART FIVE

*When Faucets Leak
and Batteries Die*

INTRODUCTION

Nothing makes a woman home alone yearn for ruffled petticoats and a strong male shoulder like a clogged toilet, dripping faucet, or dead battery.

How can a woman home alone prepare for emergencies before they happen? Chapter 24 suggests crisis questions to ask ahead of time, and a few wise preparations to make. Chapter 25 gives instructions for simple household repairs. Chapter 26 tells how to handle common automobile crises.

Also see Checklist 5, A Basic Tool Kit; Checklist 6, Home and Car Maintenance Schedule; and Checklist 7, Basic Car Supplies and Equipment.

Think of this section as a crash course on "How to Maintain a House and Car." It may be one of the most important courses you've ever taken.

It can save you money.

It may even save your life.

CHAPTER TWENTY-FOUR

What to Do Before You Have an Emergency

Lord, the carpenter said the entire beam on the carport is rotten and will have to be replaced. Is that true? Will he do a good job? Shall I trust him, or call around to look for a better deal? When things need fixing on the house, I'd like a fourth-floor condominium with maintenance included!

There are two ways a woman home alone can prepare for emergencies before they happen—which makes them less frightening and overwhelming. One is to consider how to answer crisis questions, and the other is to make a few simple preparations.

ANSWER THE CRISIS QUESTIONS

Sarah Gay remembers, "Late one evening I heard running water. My water heater is in the attic over my guest room closet, and it had sprung a leak. Water was pouring down over my off-season clothes, extra blankets, and guest room carpet. My first thought was, 'Whom do I call about this at 10 P.M.?'"

181

Other questions a woman alone may ask when facing various household or automobile crises are:

- Should I get it fixed, or wait?
- Do I dare spend all that money?
- Am I competent to handle this alone?
- Can I fix it myself?

Let's consider ways to answer those questions now, *before* there's a crisis.

Whom Do I Call?

When Sarah Gay's water heater leaked, she was lucky to have a neighbor she could call. "He knew how to turn my water off at the street—which I didn't—and then he crawled up in the attic to diagnose what was wrong." Paula calls her brother-in-law. Lauren calls her father. Allison calls her stepfather. Jill calls church members. Whom would you call? If you don't know whom to call:

1. Ask friends or church members *now* whom they recommend for different kinds of repairs; and
2. Urge your congregation to compile a list of repair people members have found reliable, and make it available to newcomers and women home alone.

A WISE WOMAN KNOWS
*Post emergency repair numbers
near the phone.*

Should I Get it Fixed, or Wait?

"When something breaks," says Lauren, "my husband is so handy, he can fix anything. But if he's not there, can it wait? And when he comes back, fixing things around the house is not a high priority in the little bit of time he has at home. I'm torn between calling somebody to fix it and knowing he could do it."

What should you do? Other women advise:

1. If you are single, go ahead and fix it as soon as you can afford to, so you don't have to worry about it anymore.

2. If you are married and he's away temporarily, you may want to wait. However, if you were out of town and this happened to him, would you want him to fix it, or leave it for you to deal with?

One way to make a decision is to use the Male Yardstick: "What would [a man you know] do about this?" Men aren't necessarily more competent, but they are often more experienced in making this sort of decision.

Do I Dare Spend the Money?

June said candidly, "Money solves a lot of crises. Knowing you can afford to buy a new appliance or call a repair person takes away a lot of stress." Susan, a teacher whose husband travels, agreed. "Knowing I can afford to pay somebody to tow the car or fix the washer makes it easier to decide to call them."

If you face a major expenditure and your budget is tight:

1. Make certain you trust the person suggesting the expenditure. Dishonest mechanics, salespersons, and repair persons may try to sell car parts you don't need and a new washer when the old one merely needs a belt. If you don't have a repair person you trust, see "Whom do I call?" above.

2. Compare prices. If buying a new product, go to the library and check *Consumer Reports'* evaluation of different brands. Can you get a good used item instead of a new one? Mechanics can often replace car parts with reconditioned ones, for example. Ask before they sell you a new one. If facing an expensive repair, it's usually wise to get a second opinion.

3. Don't fall for dire predictions. "Lady, your brakes are in such bad shape they could kill a child on your way home." Get another opinion.

4. Be as leery of a very low estimate as of a high one. We paid to repair one roof twice—once when we paid the first man to fix it, and again when we paid someone else to fix what he did wrong. Ask for an explanation of exactly what you will get for your money and what warranty comes with the work.

5. Ask for advice if you need it. Once you have an estimate, call someone who has faced a similar situation to discuss options.

6. Determine how you will pay for the repair. Putting expensive repairs and replacements on a charge card can be easy, but we can fall into financial holes by overcharging what we cannot pay within the next few months—and by failing to think of possible alternatives: buying a used item, using savings for the repair, or doing without the item for a while and saving for the repair.

7. Consider a barter. Do you know someone who might do the repair in exchange for home cooking, mending, child care, transportation, or so forth?

Am I Competent to Handle This?

Jill voiced probably the greatest concern underlying women's reluctance to handle a crisis themselves: "I don't feel quite confident about handling household repairs. We've got established repair people, but I worry whether I'm handling it as well as he would. You begin to learn, however, that you do."

Early in our marriage I discovered a closely guarded male secret: men aren't born knowing how to fix things, they just know where to go to learn how. I discovered this quite by accident . . .

When we moved into our first house, a crumbling Victorian, the city inspector condemned our unvented gas water heater. Facing the prospect of cold showers, my husband located a second-hand electric water heater. "I can put it in myself," he assured me. But to my astonishment, he headed not to pick up the water heater, tools, or supplies, but to his father's—to "read up a bit" in the *Handyman's Encyclopedia*. Bob knew no more about plumbing than I did—he was just willing to learn.

A WISE WOMAN KNOWS
*I am as competent as any man
to learn how to do this.*

Remember: competency has nothing to do with gender. It has to do with experience and confidence. If you feel incompetent to make a wise decision, review Chapter 2.

If you feel nervous about talking with repair personnel, picture yourself as the Queen of England. Speak confidently and firmly. Give your full name (yours, not the Queen's), and ask to speak with someone qualified to handle your questions. Persist! Don't explain to five or six underlings. Use simple, concise sentences, not long, rambling explanations. If you need to, write down what you want to say: "My air conditioner keeps tripping the circuit breaker." And find out right away how much something will cost—for advice or an estimate as well as for actual work.

Can I Fix it Myself?

Priscilla, whose father was a tugboat captain, remembers, "We used to freeze every year when the first cold wave came, because Mama never learned how to light the pilot light on the heater."

A woman home alone does well to learn to deal with as many situations as she can—which may be more than she thinks she can. Lyn Herrick first started fixing things when her husband was in graduate school, her apartment was decrepit, her Volkswagen ancient, and money tight. Gradually she learned that "fixing things on your own is both practical and deeply satisfying." Today she has a business doing household and automobile repairs for other women. In a helpful book on how household fixtures work and how to repair them, Herrick describes what happens to a woman who learns to cope with her own household crises:

> Not only will you be able to solve many of your own problems, but . . . even if you are unable to repair the broken object, you will have enough understanding of the problem to talk intelligently to the service person. It is more difficult for them to take advantage of you if you know what you are talking about.[1]

Martha, mother of two and married to a salesman, says, "It was bred into us that we wait for a man to do everything. We just have to get over that."

MAKE A FEW WISE PREPARATIONS

1. Buy a basic home repair book you can understand. A home repair manual is as useful to a woman home alone as a health manual! Compare several, looking up a subject like "how to fix a leaky faucet" or "how to unclog a toilet," and buy the one with explanations and illustrations you best understand. Familiarize yourself with the table of contents before you have an emergency.

The public library also has home repair books. Look in the 643.7 section for both manuals and home repair encyclopedias. One set I particularly like was published by Time Life Books and edited by people who don't presume you know a wrench from pliers or can name the parts of a toilet by heart.

2. Keep your automobile manual in your glove compartment. Read the index to learn what it contains.

3. Get fire extinguishers and smoke detectors. I repeat what I said in chapter 9: every house needs smoke detectors near bedrooms and in the kitchen. Fire departments recommend changing batteries in smoke detectors each spring and fall when the time changes. Every house also needs at least a kitchen fire extinguisher. You may want a fire extinguisher for your car, as well. We got our first extinguisher as a wedding present from a friend who was badly burned when a table lamp caught fire.

A WISE WOMAN KNOWS
Fire extinguishers are like wills.
If you don't get one until you need it,
you are too late.

Find fire extinguishers in WalMart, K-Mart, hardware stores, and even some large drug stores. Look for three things when choosing:

1. *Type.* Fire extinguishers come in four types:
   A-Type for burning wood, paper, cloth, and plastics;
   B-Type for flammable liquids like grease, oil, and paint;
   C-Type for electrical fires; and
   ABC-rated for all types of fires.
2. *Certification.* Check the label to be sure your fire extinguisher has been tested by a certified laboratory.
3. *One-use or reusable.* Some fire extinguishers must be discarded after one use; others can be recharged.

How big a fire extinguisher should you buy? If you can't easily lift it, you can't use it.

4. Find your water cutoffs. The main water cutoff for most homes is located where the water turns into your lot from the street. Look for a metal plate in your front yard. If you lift the metal plate, you will see a pipe and a meter. Between the meter and your house, you may have a valve handle, which requires a long iron "T" to cut the water off and on.

Do you know where the main water cutoff to your house is located? If not, call the water company and ask now, before you have water gushing all over the yard or kitchen floor! Do you know where your "T" is? If not, you can buy one at a hardware store.

After writing that paragraph, I realized I had never found the cutoff for our new house. I left my computer to go look, and when I lifted our metal plate, I saw a meter box full of water! The water company is already grateful I wrote this book.

I, too, am grateful I wrote this book, because our cutoff valve was not in the hole with the meter. While the water company man was here, he taught me that new houses often have a "private house valve." Ours is located at the base of our outside front spigot—where any mischievous six-year-old could cut it off, but we would have drained the city reservoir before we ever found it.

In addition to the main cutoff, small cutoffs on incoming water lines of toilets, sinks, and water heaters and some lavatories, dishwashers, and washing machines will cut off water so you can work on that line. Cutoffs on outdoor spigots let you shut off water and drain outside pipes in cold weather.

5. Find and label your electrical box. Find the box and determine which electrical circuit goes to which room or wall plugs before you need to know. Then keep a flashlight near the box.

Your box is behind a beige or gray metal door at eye level. Look in the garage, basement, closets, or even outside. We had one hidden behind a bathroom door.

To open it, pull the metal ring or plastic tab on the door. Some require a firm pull.

To label each circuit, you need another person. Get labels and an indelible pen. Turn on all overhead lights and appliances. Stand by the box and station the other person in one room at a time. Turn breaker switches off and on and ask your partner to yell when the power goes off. Make sure you know whether a circuit is for overhead lights only, or for wall plugs in the room as well. Label each circuit clearly.

If you have fuses, you will need to remove each fuse and test as described above. Keep extra fuses near the fuse box. Touch fuses *only* by the glass when screwing in or out, and do *not* put a penny in an empty fuse hole. It could cause a fire.

A WISE WOMAN KNOWS
When working with electricity,
have dry hands and a dry floor.
If the floor is damp,
stand on a board or rubber mat.

6. Assemble a basic tool kit. We aren't talking major carpentry and auto repairs here, just simple house and car maintenance, but women home alone need tools they both know how to use and how to find. If you have children, threaten to hang them by the toes if they lose your tools. *For basic tools and supplies, see Checklist 5.*

7. Get appliance manuals. These don't make any bestseller lists, but they are fascinating reading when something goes wrong. Troubleshooting instructions can save costly service calls.

If you inherited appliances without manuals when you bought a house, write or call for new ones. 1–800–555–1212 will give you the 800 number if your manufacturer has one. If they don't, ask your public library reference department for the mailing address or phone number of the company. Before writing or calling the company, have ready the model number and other information located on the appliance.

File warranties and repair receipts with manuals. Not only will this help you find them, but if you sell the house, you'll have manuals and maintenance reports for the new owners.

8. Consider changing your life to make emergencies less likely. Some women literally plan their lives to minimize household crises. Judi, a widow, and June, the working wife of a pilot, both choose to live in condominiums with a maintenance staff. June even takes a bus to work so she doesn't have to worry about automobile breakdowns.

Suzanne's family loved their isolated country home, but when her husband took a traveling job, they decided to move into town with neighbors nearby.

Frances, a retired widow, and Lynn, who has chronic fatigue syndrome and a traveling husband, both rent spare bedrooms in their homes to college students who are available for lifting, tree planting, snow shoveling, and rides if a car breaks down.

Are there changes you could make in your living situation that would cut down on the likelihood of household emergencies?

9. Set up a house, lawn, and car maintenance schedule. If you have sole or major responsibility for home and car maintenance, make a calendar of maintenance that needs to be done. Get a notebook and designate a page for each month. Jot down which plants need fertilizing or pruning, and what household routine maintenance needs to be done in each. At the beginning of each month, check the notebook and plan accordingly. *For a basic schedule, see Checklist 6.*

PERMIT YOURSELF PRIDE IN BEING PREPARED

If you have a home repair manual, fire extinguishers, an acquaintance with your water cutoffs and electrical circuits, tools you know how to use, appliance manuals, a list of competent persons you can call in an emergency, and a maintenance schedule, you are prepared for most household emergencies.

In one group interview, several women spoke of the pride they feel in solving their own emergencies. "I like to stretch my abilities," said August, mother of four and wife of a Coast Guard pilot. "When my husband's been away, I've put a doorknob back on, scraped a ceiling and repainted it, and even rewired a lamp. My kids cringed when I turned the lamp on, sure it would explode, but it didn't."

"I connected the hoses to my washer and drier after I moved," Priscilla boasted. "When I did my first wash, I was so proud!"

Master a few new household skills. When you accomplish something new, you'll feel like sending up balloons!

Suggested Further Reading

Any good home repair manual, especially:

Herrick, Lyn. *Anything He Can Fix, I Can Fix Better*. Valle Crucis, NC: Quality Living Publications, 1990. A comprehensive guide to home and auto repair, spiral-bound for easy use. Order from the publisher: P.O. Box 1, Valle Crucis, NC 28691. $12.95 including postage; proceeds benefit Habitat for Humanity.

CHAPTER TWENTY-FIVE

Coping with Common House Repairs

The following pages tell how to fix the simplest things that go wrong with a house before you waste money on a repair service call, and which other problems you can repair with instructions from your house repair book.

SAFETY FIRST!

Safety must be a prime consideration when you are doing home repairs, particularly when you are working alone. Be sure to:

1. Wear safety goggles if your eyes are in danger.
2. Wear sturdy shoes with nonslip soles.
3. Tie back long hair and remove jewelry if using power tools.
4. Never carry sharp tools in your pocket!
5. Never carry tools in your mouth.
6. Have plenty of light.
7. Keep a first-aid kit handy.
8. Make sure someone else is in shouting distance.

TOOLS AND TERMS YOU NEED TO KNOW

You will need at least a general acquaintance with a hammer, screwdrivers, drill, wrench, and a few other basic tools. *For a list of Basic Tools a woman home alone needs in her kit, see Checklist 5.* In addition to tools, there are a few terms you need to know:

Bolt: a screw with a flat end. Comes in many diameters.

Nut: round or octagonal piece that screws on a bolt.

Washer: round, but flat. Used under the head of a screw or bolt to make a tight seal. Rubber washers are used in a toilet tank and faucets to prevent leaks. When they wear out, they are easy to replace.

O-rings: washers that are plump, like tiny doughnuts.

Caulk: seals cracks around window frames, door frames, bathtubs, sinks. If ignored, these cracks let in water or air. You can buy Elmer's caulk in the same kind of bottle as Elmer's glue, making it very easy to use.

Grout: used between ceramic tiles. When grout crumbles and comes out, water gets beneath the tiles and floors or wallboard can swell, causing serious problems. Your home repair manual can tell you how to chip out the old grout and put in new. Be sure to match your original color.

Spackle, spackling compound: used to fill holes in wallboard or plaster. Premixed is much easier to use.

RULE FOR TURNING FAUCETS OR SCREWS:
Left is loose, right is tight.

TOILETS

Tip: To save water, put a brick or plastic half-gallon jug of water in the tank. This cuts down on water volume, but permits the water to fall from its regular height, giving a good flush.

Diagnosis Chart

* Instructions given in chapter.
** Not difficult with home repair manual.

Problem	Possible Cause	Solution
Stopped up	clogged with paper	plunge out*
	small object in drain	fish out*
	large object in drain	call a plumber
Tank leaks	loose bolts	tighten bolts*
	worn-out washers	replace washers*

Leaks at base	needs new seal	call a plumber
Won't flush properly	needs more water in tank	adjust water level* or adjust flush valve*
Water runs constantly	too much water in tank	adjust float ball*
	handle stuck down	adjust flush chain*
	water not staying in tank	replace flush valve*
Won't flush	worn-out mechanism	replace mechanism**

Before working on a toilet, cut off the water, turning the valve at the baseboard to the right.

Unstopping a Clogged Toilet

You flushed, and instead of going down, it came up. Maybe it even overflowed. What to do?

1. Fetch your plunger. Never use a chemical drain cleaner in your toilet. They can splash and burn you badly.
2. Scoop out solid material in the bowl (use a plastic container you can discard afterwards).
3. Using your handy plunger—which isn't called a plumber's friend for nothing—plunge vigorously a dozen times or more. If the water runs out, you've succeeded! Add water to the bowl from a bucket until it begins to flush, cut on the water, and cheer.
4. If plunging doesn't work, you've got something stuck in the drain passage—hopefully something small like a little red truck or a cloth diaper. Dip the water out, and then, because a toilet drain slants upward, use a hand mirror to try to see the obstruction. Bend a wire coat hanger straight, leaving the hook at one end, and use it to pull out the blockage. Be careful not to push the blockage farther into the drain! If you cannot see anything, you must either rent an auger (plumber's snake) and fish far down the drain, or hire a plumber.

Repairing a Leaky Toilet Tank

First, determine whether moisture on the floor beneath the toilet tank is condensation or a leak. Leaving the water turned on to the toilet, add one tablespoon food coloring to the tank water and leave the tank full. Do not flush. When moisture next appears, wipe it up with something white. (Remember, the water in the tank is clean.) If the moisture is colored, you've got a leak.

Look the tank over for a crack. If you find one, the tank will have to be replaced. Call a plumber.

If you don't have a crack, presume you need new washers or tighter bolts.

1. Cut the water off and flush to drain the tank.
2. Feel underneath the tank to locate bolts that bolt the tank to the toilet itself.
3. Take the lid off the tank and use a screwdriver to hold each bolt while you tighten the nut below with a wrench. *Turn gently and tighten only enough to stop the leak.* Toilets are made of porcelain and crack easily.

If it still leaks, you need to replace the rubber washers between the head of the nut and the tank.

1. Unscrew the bolt, lift out the nut and washer, and take the old washer to the hardware store as a model for a new one. Replace and tighten gently with a wrench, as described above.
2. If the leak is beneath the flushing mechanism, tighten the bolt beneath it while holding the flushing mechanism itself with your other hand. Be gentle!

If the water is not coming from the tank, there's a good chance it's leaking from the toilet itself. If so, you need a new seal. That's a good time to call a plumber or a plumbing friend.

When the Toilet Doesn't Flush Properly

You don't have enough water in the tank and need to raise the level, or your flush valve isn't raising high enough when you flush to let all the water out.

1. Look beneath the tank lid. Find a tube with a hole in the top. Is your water almost to the top of the tube? If not, locate the float ball (a large ball, often black or copper) attached to the rest of the mechanism by a metal arm and screw. Unscrew the ball a little to lengthen the distance between ball and shut-off valve.

2. If that doesn't work, bend the arm gently up, to raise the height of the ball so more water will flow into the tank before it cuts off. Optimally, your water level will rise almost to the top of the overflow tube.

3. If the toilet still runs, take the tank lid off, flush the toilet, and watch the small rubber flap at the bottom, attached to the handle either by a chain or a metal piece that screws into the flushing handle. The flap is called the flush valve, and should complete its rise when you push down on the handle. If it is not raising properly, adjust the length of the connecting rod or shorten the chain by changing the link that is connected to the handle.

When the Toilet Runs and Runs

If your home is filled with the music of a gently running toilet, you are wasting water.

1. The simplest problem to fix is too much water in the tank, which overflows into the overflow tube. Screw the float ball (see previous section) further into the shut-off valve to shorten it.

2. If that doesn't cut back the water enough, gently bend the arm down, to lower the height of the ball. The lower the ball, the sooner the water cuts off.

3. Another simple problem is that your flush valve chain is too taut, holding the handle up and letting water leak slowly out. To loosen, lengthen the amount of chain connecting it to the flush handle by changing links.

4. If the valve is worn out, it's easy to replace. One type has a collar that slips over the overflow tube. The other type has two hooks that hook onto the tube. Slip off or unhook, then either unhook the chain or unscrew the metal piece that connects to the handle. Remove your old valve and take it to the hardware

store for a replacement. If yours is the screw-in type, you simply screw the new one in and attach it to the overflow tube. If yours has a chain, adjust the chain so that when you pull down the handle, the valve comes up, and when lowered, the valve fits snugly.

Perhaps your toilet's entire flushing mechanism needs to be replaced. Don't despair! Look carefully at your old mechanism, then choose a kit at the hardware store that most resembles it. Each package comes with full directions. Buy a kit, get your wrench, drain the tank, and go to work. You can do it!

SINKS AND BASINS

Tip: To keep drains running free, weekly pour 1/2 cup baking soda and 1/2 cup vinegar down each drain. Allow ten minutes to settle. Pour down a kettle of boiling water to flush.

Diagnosis Chart

* Instructions given in chapter.
** Not difficult with home repair manual.

Problem	Possible Cause	Solution
Clogged drain	stuff in plug	clean plug*
	small block in pipe	plunge* or clean stopper**
	major block in pipe	call plumber
Dripping faucet	worn-out washer	replace washer*
	worn-out faucet assembly	replace assembly**
Sluggish faucet	screen clogged	unclog screen*

Before working on a sink or lavatory, cut off the water at individual cutoffs or, if you don't have them, at the street.

For Clogged Drains

Use a plumber's plunger to unblock, using effort both while pushing and while pulling. Try up to ten sets of twelve plunges each, then flush with hot tap water and use soda and vinegar treatment described above.

If the drain is still clogged, put a pan underneath the basin and take off the P-trap, that curvy piece of pipe under the basin or sink. If you are lucky, you'll have plastic pipe and can unscrew by hand the two nuts holding the P-trap in place. If you have metal pipes, use a wrench. When you get the P-trap loose, scrub it out with a toothbrush at another sink. The voice of experience says: Don't turn on the water while the P-trap is off!

For Clogged Lavatory Drains

If you don't find a clog by plunging or examining the P-trap, you need to take out the stopper. Some merely lift out. Others screw out. If yours neither lifts nor screws out, look at the assembly from underneath with a flashlight, then find its picture in your household repair manual. Once you see a diagram of how it fits together, it's simple to take apart, clean out, and reassemble.

If you try all this and still have a clog, you need a plumber's snake or, easier, a plumber.

When a Faucet Drips

You've either got worn-out washers or a worn-out faucet. Neither is very complicated to replace. However, those in a bath-tub or shower require a special wrench to reach them, so check your home repair manual for instructions.

The most common reason for leaking faucets is worn-out washers. If the dripping faucet is on a sink or lavatory, cut off your water at the supply valve, drain the pipe by turning on the faucet for a few seconds, close the drain and put a towel or face cloth in the basin to catch parts that fall, then examine your faucets.

1. Bathroom faucets have four basic parts: screw, handle, stem, and washer. Often the screw is hidden beneath plastic discs marked "H" and "C." Discs with an edge like a coin screw out; discs with smooth edges flip out if you insert a sharp knife blade beneath them.

2. Kitchen faucets come in three types: faucets with two small rubber washers under the faucet handle, washerless, and faucets with a ball assembly.

To repair faucets with small rubber washers:

1. Unscrew the screw and pry off the handle.
2. Using a wrench, unscrew the stem and look at it. There's a black rubber washer at one end that blocks water flow when the faucet is off. If it's worn or cut, water will leak through and the faucet will drip.
3. Unscrew the washer from the stem, take it to the hardware store, and buy an identical one.
4. Before reassembling the faucet, clean inside and out, using a moistened toothbrush dipped in cleanser. Scrape any sediment from openings, and sand lightly if necessary with very fine sandpaper. Rinse thoroughly.
5. Screw the new washer onto the stem, screw the stem into the sink, tighten with wrench, and replace the handle. If you still have a leak, replace the washer on the other side.

If the faucet still leaks, you will need to replace one or both valve seats. Those are the little brass rings on which the washers sit, and they may get nicked or cracked. They aren't hard to replace. Consult your home repair manual.

Repairing washerless faucets

These seldom drip, and when they do, usually have to be replaced. To remove it so you can buy an identical faucet:

1. Pry off the knob cover.
2. Unscrew the screw.
3. Pry off the handle.
4. Unscrew the stem nut with a wrench.
5. Pull out the assembly.
6. If there is a thin rubber diaphragm underneath, pry it off with a screwdriver.

Take the entire old assembly into the store to see if you can buy parts or must replace them. Instructions for replacement come on the package.

Repairing kitchen faucets with ball assembly

These are the faucets with one handle sitting on a ball that rotates from hot to cold. To repair this type of faucet is not difficult, just a bit tedious. Check your home repair manual.

Note, however, that to remove the old assembly, you will need to take out a funny-looking screw with a hexagonal hole, embedded in the faucet. That is an Allen screw, and must be removed with an Allen wrench—a bent metal rod that, in cross-section, is a hexagon. Allen wrenches come in many sizes, and you can buy a complete set inexpensively.

Or, if you plan to replace the entire faucet assembly, an Allen wrench of the correct size comes in the package.

Sluggish faucet:

If one faucet is sluggish and all others have adequate pressure, you probably just have a clogged screen in that one faucet. This can be especially true after work on pipes, either inside or outside the house.

Feel the place in the faucet where water comes out, and locate a tiny fine-mesh screen. Unscrew the head of the faucet and check the screen. If clogged, clean out and screw back onto the faucet.

PLUMBING AND HEATING

Diagnosis Chart

* Instructions given in chapter.
** Not difficult with home repair manual.

Problem	Possible Cause	Solution
Pipes: no water	pipes frozen	thaw pipes*
Furnace: no heat	gas or oil tank empty	fill tank
	gas valve off	turn gas valve on
	pilot light off	light pilot light*
	emergency switch off	turn switch on
	bad thermostat	replace thermostat**
Hot Water Heater: no hot water		
gas	pilot light off	light pilot light*
electric	power off	replace fuse* or throw circuit breaker
water too hot	thermostat too high	lower thermostat*
water too cold	thermostat too low	raise thermostat*

Preventing and Coping with Frozen Plumbing

I write this in Miami, so I have to trust the experts. They say your most vulnerable pipes are those to outside faucets and those running in unheated crawl spaces or attics and between uninsulated or poorly insulated walls. Pipes in states with few hard freezes are more likely to be vulnerable than in states that expect months of cold.

To prevent frozen pipes:

Before a freeze comes or if you are leaving for more than a week in winter months, leave water dripping from each indoor faucet. Running water doesn't freeze as easily as still water. Cut off water to outside faucets at shut-off valves, open the faucets to drain, and leave the faucets on.

When a pipe freezes:

Listen to the weather forecast. If the temperature is going up, the pipes may thaw on their own. If they don't, try the following:

1. Locate which pipes have frozen. Start with the faucets farthest from the water meter and turn on each faucet. Frozen pipes have no running water. If you can see the pipes, examine for a bulge.
2. Leave all faucets connected to the frozen pipe open so water can escape as it thaws.

Once you locate a problem spot:

1. With faucets on, use a heat lamp or a hair dryer to warm the pipe or area of wall it is behind. Always start with the part of the pipe closest to the faucet, so that as the water thaws and turns to steam, it can get out the open faucet. *Do not hit a frozen pipe, pour hot tap water on it, or attempt to thaw with a propane torch.* Frozen pipes are brittle. They may crack, burst, or even explode!

If a pipe bursts, it will drip. At that point, unless you want to learn to repair pipes, you need a plumber.

Restarting a Gas Furnace or Hot Water Heater

Pilot lights on gas furnaces and hot water heaters may blow out occasionally in a puff of wind, or be turned off for various reasons.

Instructions for relighting should be printed right above the pilot light itself. Keep long matches for this, or tear a strip of brown paper bag and twist it tightly to form a long taper. Set a bowl of water beside you as you work to douse the taper when you are done.

Important: If lighting instructions say to leave the button depressed for one minute after touching flame to gas, do so. Gas needs time to reach the flame.

If water is too hot or too cold:

Lowering a hot water heater thermostat to 120–130 degrees saves money and energy. Families with small children or an elderly member, especially, should keep the thermostat low to reduce the risk of burns.

When going away, use "vacation" setting.

The only time a thermostat needs to be at 140 or higher is when someone is ill; then raise so the dishwasher will kill contagious harmful bacteria.

On a gas water heater, the thermostat is located where the gas connection joins the tank. Turn it to the desired temperature.

Electric water heaters usually have two thermostats, one for each heating element in the tank. They are located under two removable panels on the heater, one at the top and one at the bottom. Unscrew the screws holding the panel in place and set dial to desired temperature.

Common furnace problems:

(1) a faulty thermostat, (2) a flipped circuit breaker, and (3) an empty oil drum or gas tank. For gas or oil furnaces, before you call a repairman, check the fuel level. If you have plenty of fuel and your pilot light is lit, check the thermostat by turning it off, then on and way down low to see if the furnace clicks as if it wanted to come on. If nothing clicks, you may have a faulty thermostat.

You can put in a thermostat, using your home repair manual, and save yourself a good bit of money. Just remember to turn off the power before you begin.

If the furnace flips the circuit breaker and flips it again soon after you restart the furnace or each time the furnace comes back on, you need a service call.

POWER FAILURE
Diagnosis Chart
* Instructions given in chapter.
** Not difficult with home repair manual.

Problem	Possible Cause	Solution
Lights go out in one area	Overloaded circuit	Lower the load*
	Short in circuit	Call electrician
	Short in switch	Replace switch
	Short in appliance	Repair/replace appliance

I find working with electrical systems terrifying. Follow all safety rules, and turn the power off where you are working.

Diagnose the Problem
1. Note when the power failed. If it was after lights and appliances had been on a while, you probably have an overload. If it's as soon as you switched on something, you probably have a short circuit.
2. Turn off and unplug all appliances on that circuit unless one of them is smoking. Because electricity can't get across the short, it may build up, get very hot, and cause a fire.

A WISE WOMAN KNOWS
Never touch a smoking appliance or switch!
Get out and call 911!

3. Open the fuse box or circuit panel. Have a dry floor and dry hands, and if the floor is damp, stand on a wooden board or rubber mat. Keep the rest of your body away from other objects. You do not want to become part of an electrical circuit yourself!
4. Look for the bad circuit or fuse. It should be easy to spot. If you have circuit breakers, one of the switches will have flipped itself and be out of line with the others, and may show red or white on one side. If you have fuses, one of them will have a break in the small metal strip just inside the glass, or will have actually blackened the glass.

NOTE: Fuses to big appliances like stoves and dryers are usually large cylinder cartridges. They won't look blown, so if you think it's blown, replace it.

Try a Simple Solution First

For circuit breakers, push the tripped switch to "reset" or "off" (depending on your box) and back on again. It's like turning a light switch sideways.

For fuses, pull the main switch to turn off all your power, and replace the blown fuse (the one with a break in the internal wire). If the breaker does not trip or the fuse does not blow immediately, you probably had an overload. Unplug some appliances from that circuit.

If the breaker trips or the fuse blows immediately, you probably have a short circuit, an interruption in the electricity somewhere along the line in a switch, wiring, appliance, or lamp.

To Check Internal Wiring and Switches

Unplug all appliances and turn off all wall switches, then turn the circuit breaker back on. If it fails at once, your short is in the wiring and you need an electrician.

If the power does not fail at once, flip wall switches one by one. *A defective switch will trip the circuit breaker again, and needs replacing.* Call an electrician or repair the switch yourself, using your home manual. If you repair it yourself, be cautious and follow all safety instructions.

FAULTY APPLIANCES

If Wall Switches Do Not Trip the Circuit

Look for a faulty appliance. Examine all plugs and cords for a cut or nick in the rubber coating. Wrap nicks in cords with electrical tape or replace the faulty plug (instructions on plug package).

If you cannot see an obvious cause of a short, buy a "continuity tester" from a hardware store and test appliances individually.

Do not use any appliance until certified in good condition!

Electrical Danger Signals

Sparks at a switch or light. Turn off with a thick towel or heavy glove and call electrician.

Smoke or fire. GET OUT! CALL 911 AND THEN AN ELECTRICIAN!

REPAIRING A HOLE IN THE WALL

You've moved several pictures, gouged a wall moving the piano, watched a crack develop along a wall while your old house settled, thrown something against a wall in fury, or come home to discover your kids chiseling away plaster hoping to find a secret room—as ours once did. Do not despair!

1. Fetch the spackling compound and a putty knife.
2. Dust the wall and scrape away any loose plaster along a crack by running the corner of your putty knife along it. Repairing a small hole or crack is merely a matter of scooping a little spackling compound onto your putty knife and smoothing it into the hole, being sure to remove extra that gets on the wall surface itself.

Repairing a hole up to two inches in diameter or deeper than 1/4 inch requires skill and patience, but is not hard. Simply fill a bit, let it dry, then fill more and let it dry, until it's done. Allow it to harden, then sand gently with very fine sandpaper until smooth. Large holes (more than two inches) require more work. Consult your home repair manual.

FIXING ROOF LEAKS

If the leak is a small one and you are reasonably agile, you can fix a roof yourself.

1. If all you have is a curled shingle, buy a small amount of roofing cement in a tube, smear it onto area beneath the curled shingle, press down, and put a brick on the spot for an hour or two until it dries.
2. If you have an obvious hole, fill it with roofing cement, cut a patch from a matching shingle, press it over the hole, and cover

the entire patch and for about one inch beyond with more roofing cement.

3. If you have a cracked or torn asphalt shingle, you will need to replace not only the cracked shingle, but probably several others as well. Consult your home repair manual.

4. For flat or tile roof repairs, check your manual.

A Few Roofing Cautions

1. If your roof is tile, cedar shakes or shingles, or very steep, call a professional. Your neck is far more important than your roof.

2. If your home repair manual tells you to drain accumulated water above a ceiling by drilling holes in the ceiling, use a cordless drill or make the holes by hammering a screwdriver into the ceiling. Drilling into a wet ceiling with an electric drill can be fatal.

3. Don't *ever* try to repair a roof when you are home alone. At the very least, invite a friend to watch her favorite TV program within hailing distance while you work.

WASHER PROBLEMS

Diagnosis Chart

* Instructions given in chapter.
** Not difficult with home repair manual.

Problem	Possible Cause	Solution
Won't agitate, spin or drain	not plugged in	plug in
	fuse blown; circuit off	replace or reset (see p. 202-203)
Fills too slowly	hose kinked	straighten hose
	hose clogged	clean hose screens*
Agitates, won't spin	load off balance	redistribute clothes equally
Won't agitate	broken or loose drive belt	replace or tighten belt*
Won't fill at all	faucets off	open both faucets
	solenoid defective	service call
	timer defective	service call

If the Washer Won't Fill or Fills Too Slowly

Follow each hose from machine to fauet, and if there's a kink, unkink it. If you don't find a kink, a hose may be blocked. At the end of each hose is a tiny screen that can get clogged with lint or water minerals.

1. Turn off the water into each hose.
2. Unscrew the hoses from the faucets. Look inside the opening for the screen.
3. Remove the screen and clean off. Reinsert screen and reconnect the hoses. Do not overtighten. Turn water back on.
4. If water still fills slowly, check the other end of each hose.
5. If this does not work, your pipes are clogged elsewhere, or your solenoid or timer are defective. You need a repair person.

If the Machine Won't Agitate

If your machine is filling with water but not agitating, chances are that its belt needs tightening. To determine if the belt is loose, place your thumb on the belt and press. If it gives more than half an inch, it needs tightening. It's not hard to do. Consult your home repair manual for instructions.

DRYER PROBLEMS

Diagnosis Chart

* Instructions given in chapter.
** Not difficult with home repair manual.

Problem	Possible Cause	Solution
Won't start	unplugged	plug in
	fuse blown,	replace fuse,
	circuit off	reset breaker*
		(see page 202-203)
	door open	close door
	not set	set properly
	defective timer	service call
Won't heat	fuse or circuit blown	replace or reset
		(see page 202-203)

	heating element burned out	service call or replace**
(if gas)	pilot light out	light pilot light (see p. 200-201)
Won't tumble	broken or loose drive belt	tighten or replace**
Takes too long to dry clothes	clogged exhaust duct	clear or unkink duct
	clogged lint screen	clean lint screen
	dryer overload	remove some clothes

HOT WATER HEATER PROBLEMS
Diagnosis Chart

* Instructions given in chapter.
** Not difficult with home repair manual.

Problem	Possible Cause	Solution
Water too hot or cold	thermostat set wrong	reset thermostat (see page 201)
Water cold or lukewarm		
(if electric)	heating element burned out	replace** or service call
(if gas)	pilot light out	relight (see p. 200-201)
Heater leaking	tank rusted out	buy new one

GARBAGE DISPOSAL PROBLEMS
Diagnosis Chart

* Instructions given in chapter.
** Not difficult with home repair manual.

Problem	Possible Cause	Solution
Won't run	jammed by bone, rind, etc.	unjam, reset*
Sluggish	clogged with grease	pour boiling water to melt

To Unjam a Garbage Disposal

1. Turn off the power.
2. Stick your hand inside the unit and feel very carefully around the cutting blade. Remove any rinds or hard objects.

3. Locate the reset button under the sink on the disposal motor. Reset this button before turning the unit back on.
4. If your unit is old and gets jammed often, keep a long-handled wooden spoon handy and use it to turn the unit without turning on the power. You may also spray with WD–40 (see Checklist 5).

DISHWASHER PROBLEMS
Diagnosis Chart
* Instructions given in chapter.
** Not difficult with home repair manual.

Problem	Possible Cause	Solution
Won't start	fuse or circuit out	replace, reset (see p.202-203)
	door not shut tightly	shut door
	control not on START	reset control
	defective switch, timer, or solenoid	service call
Overflowing	clogged strainer	clean out strainer*
Dishes not clean	water not hot enough	reset water heater to 140 (see page 201)
	strainer clogged	clean out strainer*
Noisy	vibration due to imbalance	adjust feet to level**
Not drying	water temperature too low	reset water heater to 140 (see page 201)
	defective heating element	service call
	faulty timer	service call

To Unclog a Dishwasher Strainer
1. Remove the bottom dish tray.
2. Locate strainer in bottom of dishwasher, beneath the heating element.
3. Examine to see how strainer is held in place. Some are screwed in, others are made of flexible plastic to pop in and out.
4. Remove the strainer and clean with a brush. Rinse, and replace.

ICEMAKER PROBLEMS

Diagnosis Chart

* Instructions given in chapter.
** Not difficult with home repair manual.

Problem	Possible Cause	Solution
Won't make ice	power surge or failure	turn dial to reset, hold a moment, turn to normal setting
	frozen water supply line (test by feeling tray where ice formed; if no water or ice, it is frozen)	defrost freezer, thaw line; if still won't make ice, service call

ELECTRIC STOVE PROBLEMS

Diagnosis Chart

* Instructions given in chapter.
** Not difficult with home repair manual.

Problem	Possible Cause	Solution
Oven heats improperly	burned out element	replace element**
Burners won't heat	circuit breaker off	reset breaker (see page 202-203)
One burner won't heat	burned out	replace*

To Replace a Burner on an Electric Stove

Before you do this, turn off the circuit breaker to the stove or take out the fuses.

1. Lift up the element. Remove the chrome ring.
2. Some burners merely plug in. Grasp and pull out gently. Take to the store for a replacement.
3. Some burners attach to the stove by a small screw. Remove the screw and pull gently to expose the wires.

4. Get paper and pencil and diagram how the wires are attached. Mark each wire with clearly marked masking tape so you'll remember which is which. Disconnect wires. Buy a new element.

5. Reconnect the wires per your diagram.

CHAPTER TWENTY-SIX

Coping
with a Cranky Car

Maybe some women love to lie under an automobile or bend over its hood. The only thrill I've ever gotten from automobile maintenance was the first few times I was permitted to pump my own gas. Swaggering boys had fooled me into thinking it was fun!

However, any woman home alone needs to know where her car owner's manual is (in the glove compartment?) and a few basics about automobiles, in order to keep them running properly and to avoid being taken advantage of by unscrupulous mechanics. *Checklist 7 lists basic supplies to keep in your car and in the garage.*

This chapter covers basic car maintenance and repair. For women who would like to know even more—and save more money on car repairs—most technical schools offer a car repair course.

CHECKING VITAL SIGNS

To function properly, a car—like a human being—needs enough air, water, fuel, and body fluids. By checking these periodically you can save yourself enormous repair bills.

Checking Tire Pressure

Tires with too little or too much air wear unevenly and more quickly than tires with correct pressure. To check tire pressure you need a tire gauge, available from auto supply stores or racks in drugstores, WalMart, K-Mart, and so on.

1. In your automobile manual, look up "tire pressure" to determine how much pressure your tires should hold.
2. On the tire, locate the valve where air is pumped in (a little rubber piece sticking out of the tire near the hubcaps). Screw off the cap. The gauge head is shaped to fit over this valve. Press down quickly, and a little measuring stick will shoot out the bottom of the gauge, telling you how many pounds of pressure you have in the tire. Take a couple of readings to be sure you are getting a correct one.
3. Compare your gauge reading with ideal tire pressure.
4. If you have too little air, go to the air hose of a filling station. Remove the valve cap, press the air hose to the valve, and let in air a little at a time. *Be careful not to put in too much air and burst the tire*. Add a little, check the pressure with your gauge, and add a bit more until you have enough.
5. If you have too much air, press the gauge to the valve quickly several times to release spurts of air, then take a new reading.

Checking the Tread on Tires

From time to time, check the tread on your tires. Tires with worn or slick treads slide on wet surfaces and go flat easier than good tires. There is a wear bar on all tires, a raised section of tread located in several places around the tire. It becomes bald before the rest of the tread. When it gets smooth all the way across, you need new tires.

Checking Vital Fluids

1. Checking and adding oil: Oil keeps car parts from rubbing against one another and grinding one another down. It is vital! Checking the oil should be done routinely every few gas fill-ups.

1. Get a paper towel or tissue.
2. Lift the hood of your car. For some cars that means pressing a lever near the driver's seat. If that only pops the hood part way up, you will need to feel in the crack between hood and car for another lever that shoves to one side. This will release the hood so you can raise it. (If you have trouble getting the hood up the first time, don't be proud—ask someone for help.)
3. If your hood doesn't stay up by itself, locate a propping rod on the right side of the engine. It fits into a hole on the underside of the hood. Be sure it is secure before you let go of the hood!
4. Look for the oil dip stick, a thin metal rod with a handle on the end. Pull it out and wipe it clean.
5. Reinsert it in its hole and make sure it's all the way down. Pull it back out and read the end. There are lines to show if your oil is empty, half full, or full. You may want to take two readings.
6. If you have no oil on the stick, you need two quarts of oil. If your oil is merely low, you need one quart. Check your auto manual for preferred weight, which means thickness. Different climates or seasons may vary the weight you need, but the most common are 10–40 and 10–30. You can buy oil cheaper at auto parts stores than at filling stations. Ask for it by weight: "I'd like some 10–40 oil, please." Buy several quarts and keep them handy.
7. Locate the place in your engine to pour in the oil, which is clearly marked "Oil." Unscrew the cap and lay right beside the hole so you don't forget to put it back on. Oil comes in bottles with convenient spouts, and many stations give you a paper funnel for easy pouring. If a little gets on the engine, it will smoke, but cause no damage.
8. Be sure to have the oil and oil filter changed regularly at least every 5000 miles unless your manual indicates otherwise.

  2. Checking and adding coolant: The radiator keeps your engine cool while it runs by circulating a mixture of water and coolant through engine parts. This water needs to be checked from time to time and topped up with coolant. Do this when the engine is cool.

1. Lift the hood. Locate the water overflow reservoir, which should be clearly marked. Older cars do not have one of these; they merely have a cap to unscrew on top of the radiator. If uncertain, consult your auto manual.
2. The reservoir should be full to the proper line—or, if you do not have a reservoir, the radiator should be full to within an inch or two of the top. If not, top up with coolant. You can buy gallons of coolant at auto supply stores or auto sections of stores like K-Mart and WalMart.

3. Checking your battery: The battery provides the electricity that keeps the car going. Many batteries are sealed and you don't have to worry about adding water. If you have one with plastic tops that pop off, check its fluid by removing the tops and peering inside. If the water is not up to the top, add water. Distilled water is good, but not necessary. Be careful not to let battery water get onto your skin or clothes—it is actually acid, and burns.

4. Checking brake, power steering, and transmission fluids, and windshield washer liquid: These four fluids have to be topped up from time to time. The caps to these reservoirs should be clearly marked on your engine. If not, consult your car manual. Buy the correct fluid at an auto parts store.

COPING WITH COMMON CRISES

Nothing is quite so frustrating as having a car problem on the road. Knowing how to deal with some of them, however, makes it a bit easier.

1. If your oil light ever goes on: *STOP THE CAR IMMEDIATELY.* Get assistance. Do not drive it! You may be out of oil, which can permanently damage the engine.

2. If your temperature light comes on: Your car is overheating. You are out of water or coolant.

1. Drive slowly to a water source—filling station, home, etc. Warning: Do *not* take the radiator cap off if the car is overheating! You can get badly burned!
2. Raise the hood and wait until it cools. What water there is inside the car is currently steam, and boiling hot.

3. After the radiator has cooled a bit, use a rag or old towel to turn the cap slightly, just enough to let steam escape. Be careful! You can get badly burned.

4. When the radiator stops steaming, remove the cap. Turn on your engine before putting in water, because cold water can crack a hot radiator or even an engine block.

5. Using a hose, bucket, or milk jug, fill the radiator with water while the engine is running. This permits water to fill not only the radiator, but the entire engine. Fill to the full line on your reservoir or to within an inch of the top of the radiator. Consult your manual for the recommended mix of water and coolant.

3. If you have a leak under the car: Manufacturers wisely make transmission fluid red, power steering fluid light yellow, brake fluid clear, windshield washer fluid blue, and oil brown. If you see a damp spot under your car after the air conditioner has been running, chances are it's just condensation. However, if you see a damp spot after the car's been sitting all night, blot it with a white paper towel or place white paper under the car overnight. You can determine from the color what is leaking. Then you can speak with some knowledge to your mechanic.

4. If your weather stripping gaskets come loose: Weather stripping gaskets are those rubbery things around each door that keep water and air from creeping in. From time to time they loosen. At an auto supply store, K-Mart, WalMart, etc., buy weather stripping adhesive. Follow simple instructions.

5. If your rearview mirror falls off: Sometime in the recent past car manufacturers started gluing mirrors to the windshield instead of screwing them to the car frame. Naturally, with all the handling most of them get, they eventually fall off. Buy mirror-mount adhesive to reattach the mirror. Follow the instructions.

CHANGING A FLAT TIRE

This is probably the crisis women dread the most. The idea that little old me has to jack up that great big machine is enough to fill anybody with dread—until you realize that the jack does most of the work.

Some women carry a portable inflator or a can of "quick-sealant" in their trunks for a quick repair until they can get the car to a service station.

If your tire has a big hole, or you don't have a portable inflator or can of sealant, you will need to change the tire. The chances of your having this book along when you have a flat are pretty slim, but your automobile manual will also have complete instructions. Still, you might want to practice once in your driveway.

1. Pull slowly to a safe place on the side of the road, away from a curve, and on a level surface. If you have to drive a short distance, don't worry about ruining the tire; that's less important than your life. If it is dusk, dawn, or dark, light flares behind and in front of the vehicle.

2. Consult your owner's manual. It will tell you where to find the jack, handle, and lug wrench to twist off the nuts holding on the tire, and where to find the spare tire. It may also indicate a special part of the car frame built to hold the jack. Assemble the tools and spare tire.

3. Place the jack so it will not slip, near the tire and beneath a sturdy part of the car frame. On mud or gravel, put a board, several thicknesses of brown paper bag, etc. under the jack to keep it steady.

4. Put a standard transmission car into gear and an automatic transmission car into park and put on the emergency brake.

5. Insert jack handle into jack and pump the handle until the jack is firmly against the car frame. Don't raise it yet!

6. If you have a hubcap, use the flat end of the lug wrench to pry it off. Loosen nuts holding the tire in place by turning them counterclockwise (from right to left over the nut), but don't take them completely off yet. This can be the hardest part. Tire companies often use automatic wrenches to put nuts on, which makes them almost impossible to loosen by hand. If this is the case, you will need to seek muscular aid.

7. If you succeed in loosening the nuts, raise the wheel by pumping the jack handle up and down. As you pump, thank God for

laws of physics that permit even a one hundred pound woman and a jack to lift a heavy car!

8. When the tire is several inches clear of the ground, remove the lug nuts and place them in your hubcap to keep them together.

9. Pull the tire off. Never place your legs or other parts of your body under the car while working!

10. Align the holes in the spare tire with the bolts and put it on. Put the lug nuts back on: put on one, tighten slightly, put on the next, and tighten it slightly. When all are on, go back around and tighten each a little more. Finally go around a third time, but do not yet have them completely tight. This balances the wheel better.

11. Lower the jack by using the switch to reverse the jack. When you pump, the car will come down.

12. Tighten the lug nuts completely, a bit on each one at a time until they are all tight. Don't bother to put back on the hubcap.

13. Take the flat tire to a mechanic for repair or replacement.

JUMP-STARTING A DEAD BATTERY

This is the most common problem drivers are likely to face. You turned on your lights, got out of the car, and forgot them. Or maybe the water has leaked out of your battery. Fortunately, if you have jumper cables, you can recharge the battery.

Jumper cables are long rubber-coated wires with copper clamps on both ends. They take a charge from a good battery and carry it to a dead one. Sometimes a battery will retain a charge for months afterwards. If the battery is old, it will hold the charge at least long enough to get you to the store to buy a new one.

1. Find another car with a good battery and a willing driver. Check to see where each battery is located.

2. Place the car with the good battery hood to hood with your car, with the batteries close to one another. (If batteries are on the same side, your cars will need to be off-center.)

3. Hook one red clamp to the positive (+) post of the good battery and the other red clamp to the positive (+) post of the dead battery.

TO REMEMBER WHICH CABLE IS WHICH:
Red is a POSITIVE color.

4. Hook one black clamp to the negative (-) post of the good battery. Hook the other black clamp either to the negative (-) post of the dead battery or, better, ground it by attaching it to a metal part of your car frame.
5. Stand back from your car! A bad battery can explode!
6. Ask the other driver to start his car. When that car is running, try to start your engine. If you succeed (and you probably will), leave your engine running and disconnect the cables in reverse order: black from your car, black from the other car, red from your car, red from the other car.
7. Note: Do *not* touch red and black together while connected to the running engines, or they will spark.
8. If your battery is old, replace it as soon as you can. You don't want to make a habit of this!

CLEANING A CAR

Washing a car is simple these days—just run through an automatic car wash.

A few tips for special problems:

1. Clean grease and grime off windshields with vinegar water.
2. Neutralize white salt stains on carpet with vinegar and warm water.
3. Buff out minor scratches with a mild household abrasive polish.
4. Absorb bad odors with small boxes of baking soda under the front seat and in the trunk (poke holes in lid).
5. Clean vinyl upholstery with household cleaners like 409 and Fantastik, or with cleaner especially designed for vinyl.
6. Before vacuuming, club dust from upholstery seats with a small baseball bat.
7. Use standard carpet and upholstery cleaner to clean seats and carpet.

PART SIX

Learning to Thrive

CHAPTER TWENTY-SEVEN

How to Get
the Help You Need

The first stage of learning to thrive is learning to meet our own needs. That's what earlier chapters of this book have been about. The second stage of learning to thrive is asking for help when we need it. That's what this chapter is about. And while I will talk a lot in this chapter about asking local congregations for help, what I have to say can be applied to businesses and neighborhood organizations. Some probably even applies to men alone, too.

As a woman home alone you manage a household, maintain an automobile, care for your own needs, serve as the backbone of a church or volunteer organization, hold down a full-time job, and/or raise children. You cannot, however, meet all your own needs or handle all your own crises. Superwoman is a fictitious character.

Biblically, the people of God have always been urged to care for women home alone; widows are mentioned many times as deserving special treatment. Currently, churches often go to heroic lengths to care for members when they know about a need. In *Young Widow*, Kate Convissor describes the many ways her congregation reached out to her in the months after her husband died. She declares, "Kindness with a human face meant the most."[1]

In her interview, Jill said, "When I was bedridden for many weeks, our congregation literally did everything: cooked, cleaned, came and got our laundry. When my husband had to go out of town, they even came and bathed my little ones and put them to bed. If they hadn't, I couldn't have made it. When I started losing my hair, a prayer group came to the house to pray with me." She concludes with an important sentence: "I let them know my needs, and they met them."

The apostle James once chided the early church, "You have not because you ask not" (James 4:2). That's often true for women home alone, too. But while any woman home alone can name significant ways her own congregation, community, or business could help her, most won't ask. One woman said she would appreciate child care for all meetings and someone to check in with when she drove home alone late at night after church, but added, "I feel like such a wimp! I can't expect them to do that just for me."

Perhaps not. But what if your "personal" needs are shared by large numbers of other women?

A WISE WOMAN KNOWS
Although nobody else is in my boat,
many other people are sailing the same waters.

LOOK AROUND YOU

Women home alone make up a majority of members in many communities, businesses, and congregations—and their numbers are growing. Consider, for instance: "Between 1987 and 1990, when the number of people over fifty-five rose by 2 percent, the widowed, divorced, or separated women among them rose by a whopping 37 percent."[2]

The trouble is, nobody sees them—not even other women home alone. Frequently when I interviewed several women from the same congregation and mentioned other women on my schedule, I'd get an astonished "*She's* not home alone!" Single, widowed, or divorced women had not realized how alone a woman is when her husband leaves every Monday and returns on Friday, works twenty-four-hour shifts, or is constantly on call. Childless women had never thought of single mothers as "home alone," but as one single mother said, "When you are the only parent and have to make all the decisions, you'd better believe you're alone!"

Women unwilling to ask their congregations to help them, therefore, need to realize that in doing so, they can also bring about changes to benefit other women home alone. How can you go about asking for help you need?

1. Identify your allies. Choose two or three other women home alone—perhaps one without a spouse and one with a husband who travels—who may be willing to work on this issue.

2. Gather to share your concern. Invite them to meet with you, and let them know you aren't trying to start a "group" in the church—most churches already have enough groups. Instead, suggest that you are wanting a short-term task force to consider special needs of women home alone. Ask them to name just a few of the things they themselves wish the church would do for women home alone.

3. Name other women home alone. Together, compile a list of *all* women home alone in your congregation. Include women who are single, divorced, widowed, or married to men who are: in the military, firefighters, police officers, truckers, doctors, nurses, pilots, airline stewards, in jail, sales representatives, corporate executives, professional athletes, entertainers, musicians, church or missions executives, politicians, required to work swing shifts. You will probably be astonished at the length of your list!

You might also want to list single, widowed, or divorced men and those married to women who have the jobs listed above. Men home alone have many of the same needs as women home alone.

4. Consider how to approach your pastor. As with any congregational concern, you will need the pastor's support. Discuss how best to achieve this. Be sure to point out to the pastor that these people you want to serve are not "needy" people—many may be leaders in the congregation. But their life situation causes them to have special needs, and there are ways the church could make their lives easier with simple ministries of love.

5. Consider how to best reach the women to ask what they need. Would women come to a potluck dinner at someone's home? to a church dessert? could child care be provided? You may envision a one-time asking session, a series of small groups meeting to gather information, or even, initially, a questionnaire.

6. You may want to provide resources to the congregation: a study of some portion of this book, for instance, or an adult study on biblical concern for "widows and orphans." Teale said, with a chuckle, "Last time my husband was on a missions trip, a kind man in our congregation invited me and my sons out to Sunday dinner with his family. He said he wanted to care for a widow and her orphans." That's scripturally sound!

7. Decide who will do what, by when, and when you will meet again. Come up with an action plan so that your ideas don't die at the planning stage.

NAME YOUR NEEDS

One of the questions I asked in interviews was "What are some of the toughest parts of being home alone? What could the church do to make those parts easier?"

Answers seemed to fall into three categories: personal ministries by individual church members, things that groups such as Men of the Church or youth groups can do, and congregational policies that make it easier for women both to live at home alone and to be a part of the congregation.

As an example of a personal ministry, Paula mentioned how touched she was by church members who brought her a load of firewood one winter.

Two examples of ministries by one group within the church: Diane told of a church men's group that offered a "Car Clinic" one Saturday a month to change oil and rotate tires for people in the church who didn't know how to do that, and Priscilla remembered a "Hard Hat Club" of churchmen who went out once a month in teams to do simple house repairs for women alone, particularly the elderly and those in financial straits. Each group charged for materials and supplies; donations above that went to missions.

Sarah Gay suggested a congregational ministry: "I wish the church kept a list of good mechanics and household repair people. Just knowing who someone else in the church had found reliable would help. And it would help if the church directory listed who in the congregation is a mechanic, electrician, or plumber. I never know how to find somebody I can trust."

As you ask the women home alone in your congregation to name their own needs, you may want a starting place. Here are some ideas suggested by women I interviewed. Obviously not every church needs or can do all of these, but are any of them appropriate for yours?

Personal Friendship Ministries

1. Invitations to share a meal.
2. Shared food, like stew, soup, muffins—things a woman home alone won't cook.
3. Invitations to go to a play, concert, or movie.
4. Phone numbers of people it's okay to call at any hour with an emergency.
5. Network of "check-in" partners who call one another daily to keep in touch.
6. An afternoon of child care to provide a mother alone some relief.
7. Phone calls during the week just to say hello.
8. Invitations for children to play, to give Mom a break.

Men's Group Ministries

1. Big Brother Days to share skills with children in the congregation, particularly children with an absent dad: take them fishing or to sporting events, set up a softball game, teach them to do simple carpentry or even to fly a kite!
2. Car clinic once a month to change oil, rotate tires, do small maintenance; charge for parts and materials, donations go to missions.

3. Hard Hat Club to go in teams to offer women alone assistance with moving furniture, cleaning out gutters, hanging curtains, adding ceiling fans, small repairs; again, charge for materials, donations go to missions.
4. Skills directory listing people in the church with particular expertise who are willing to be called in case of emergency.

Youth Group Ministries
1. Slave crew once each season to rake, edge, clean out gutters, wash windows, trim shrubbery; earn money for missions or camp.
2. Mothers Shopping Morning near Christmas; provide child care at the church for a Saturday morning to give single mothers time to shop; can be a service project to raise money for missions.
3. Red Cross baby-sitting training class for youth, then provide list of trained youth willing to baby-sit.
4. Weekday child-care mornings during summer to give moms a break.

Congregation-Wide Ministries
1. Child care for all meetings.
2. Early meetings for women who have to drive home alone.
3. Networks of buddies who call one another when they get home from meetings.
4. Inclusive social events: open to both couples and people alone.
5. Care teams to provide meals and other services during illness or other stress.
6. Sunday lunch club that goes out to dinner, Dutch treat, after church.
7. Reliable repair persons list maintained in church office, of mechanics and house repair services members use and have found reliable.
8. Loaner car: extra car owned by church or congregational member, available for short-term use while a car is being repaired.
9. Baby-sitter's list of responsible church youth available for baby-sitting.
10. House sitter's list of members willing to check mail, water plants, feed pets, or even stay in a vacant house.

11. Good Samaritan phone list: members who are willing to be called at any hour with medical, automotive, or household emergencies.

12. Emergency numbers service: Urge members with no in-town relatives to give out-of-town relatives the number of the church office or one congregational member to call in case of emergency; might even have a person or committee designated to hold emergency house keys.

13. Support for travelers: occasional get-togethers for couples in which one person travels, to share concerns and support; also a list of persons or churches in other cities where travelers can visit and find a welcome.

BEGINNING TO ASK

As I said in Chapter 1, women home alone are invisible. And because the church may not know how to help them, most congregations are content to let them stay invisible. One pastor admitted, "My parish is now fifty percent single. I sympathize with them and empathize with them, but I have nothing to say to them."[3]

A WISE WOMAN KNOWS
*Others cannot read my mind
about what I want or need.
I need to let them know.*

Women I interviewed spoke of weeks alone sick when nobody called, car breakdowns when nobody stopped, and being almost overwhelmed by their children with no relief. A friend whose husband has traveled for twenty years said, "In all those years, not one person in the church has asked if I needed anything while he was away."

Her husband added, "Yet when the preacher goes away, we pray for him and his family's safety. I wish the church would pray for me and my family while we're apart." He paused, then added, "Of course, I've never asked them to pray for us. . . ."

1. Decide whom to ask in the church. Once women home alone in your congregation have identified some practical ways the congregation could help women home alone, consider who are the proper persons to approach with various lists. Decide who will ask whom, when. Draw up a written list of requests, naming who is making the requests and why. If possible, suggest several alternatives and rank them in order of your own preference.

2. In addition, begin to ask for help from other women home alone. One of the things women do best is supporting one another through conversation, prayer, and just "being there." I interviewed one trio of women—a widow, a divorcée, and a politician's wife—who said, "We three have different problems, but because we're all often alone and have children nearly the same ages, we have a common thread. We pick right up on one another's needs."

Women alone in a congregation can form networks to share meals, transportation, and child care; to provide security buddies and friends to call in case of emergency; to care for one another when sick and comfort one another in grief.

The group of women least likely to have others they call on for support is women with traveling husbands. Be sure to invite them to join in outings, meals, and networks.

IN CONCLUSION

Women home alone make up a large percentage of any congregation. While many of them are active in congregational life, they share some common needs the congregation can meet—if encouraged to do so. As you consider whether or not to approach your congregation to ask them to care for their women home alone, remember: No need ever gets met without somebody getting passionate about it. Who can get more passionate than one who understands the need?

CHAPTER TWENTY-EIGHT

Cause for Celebration

While being alone might not be a first choice for most women, women home alone readily acknowledge some benefits:

"No snoring!"

"I can rent a romantic movie and cry if I want to."

"I can watch what I want to on television without somebody channel surfing."

"My house doesn't get as dirty as other people's."

"I can go out of town if I want to."

"I can read late with the lights on and nobody complains."

Sarah Gay put it succinctly: "Doing what you want to do when you want to, not doing what you don't want to do, and peace and quiet at the end of the day."

Paula seconded that: "Glorious tranquillity after a busy day!"

Whether a woman sees being alone as cause to cry or celebrate largely depends on what she chooses to focus on. In addition to the mini-celebrations above, being alone offers a woman major opportunities to celebrate. We've mentioned most of them in passing in other chapters, but let's count those blessings again.

CELEBRATE SPACE TO STRETCH OUT IN

Years ago in *A Room of One's Own*, Virginia Woolf argued that every woman needs a room that is entirely hers, to do with as she likes. Most married women do not have such a space. I recently urged a friend of mine who was writing in her guest room to redefine the room so that guests sleep in her study. She called afterwards and said, "You can't imagine what a difference that has made!" Redefining the room hasn't changed its function, but it has changed how she chose to arrange the furniture and what she chose to hang on the walls. More important, it influenced how she relates to that space: it is hers, instead of other people's that she invades to work in.

Women home alone—even married ones—have more space than other married women. They can stretch out in bed and hog all the pillows. They can spread out all over the den or dining- room table. Suzanne does craft projects. Allison does smocking and cross-stitch. Both said they don't feel as comfortable spreading projects around the house when their husbands are home as when they are gone.

June got more specific. "I like to dress dolls, so when he's away I fill up the dining-room table for four or five days at a time. Once I got a lot of misformed dolls and some fabric. I took the dolls completely apart, remade them, and dressed them. They filled up the whole house! I'd have hesitated taking that on if he'd been at home, and I was glad that week, at least, he wasn't."

CELEBRATE TIME TO PURSUE
YOUR OWN INTERESTS

Women home alone can also stretch their minds and their abilities. Lori suggested, "Being alone gives you time to try something new. You can take a class—aerobics or something at the university—whenever it's convenient for you, without worrying about when somebody else needs to eat or will be coming home." Judi went back for her master's degree after her husband died, and took pride in paying for it herself. "I needed to do something to feel good about myself, something productive."

Brenda said frankly, "The good part about being alone is the freedom to follow your own schedule and whims without interference from another adult. I wouldn't want it all the time, but once in a while it's nice. Dinner early, Brussels sprouts or TV dinners, and nobody to channel graze during your favorite programs. For that matter, days without TV at all. When my husband is gone, I stay up later and accomplish more."

June agreed. "I welcome our time apart. That's the time when I schedule things he doesn't like to do. For instance, he doesn't like to shop, so my daughter and I shop while he's away. Also, we go out to eat at places he doesn't like, or go to movies we like that he wouldn't. I also do a lot of reading and volunteer work when he's away."

A WISE WOMAN KNOWS
You are never alone
if you enjoy your own company.

CELEBRATE TIME FOR OTHERS

Paradoxically, one advantage of being alone is that we have more time and freedom for other people. We can lunch with a sister, take a child out to dinner, rock on the porch through a twilit evening with a friend and a tall cool drink. We have more time for telephone calls, church work, and volunteering.

CELEBRATE YOUR OWN POWER!

Power is a maligned word in our society, often associated with overbearing men in business suits. However, Webster's Seventh Collegiate Dictionary defines power as "possessing control, authority, or influence over others" or—I like this one—"ability to act or produce an effect."

Being alone forces us to try new things, some of which affect our own lives and many of which influence the lives of others. Each new achievement builds confidence in our ability to do more. When you feel confidence flowing through your veins, Woman, you are feeling your power!

Lauren enjoys power over her own schedule when she's alone. "It's easier to get into a routine when he is gone. When he comes home, we have to wait dinner on him or keep the child up waiting for him to get home. It seems like when he's here, we spend a lot of time waiting for him. When we're alone, time is easier to manage."

Priscilla is delighted to have power over household appliances. "When I moved, I connected my washer myself. The first time I did a wash, I was thrilled. It worked!"

Take time, for a moment, to name every way that you get to call your own shots and make your own rules when you are alone. List some skills you developed that you might not have if you had someone around to do things for you. Just for a moment, bask in the powerful person you are becoming because of having to spend so much time as a woman home alone.

Being in control of our lives—being able to imagine and take steps to shape our own lives in ways that make us happy, competent, and fulfilled—is one gift God gives to women home alone.

Paula, however, adds one word of caution: "After you've gotten used to looking out for yourself, it's easy to have less patience with people who call you for trifles. You expect them to be able to stand on their own two feet, too—and you don't want to give them your time. As we develop our own abilities, it's important to remember that other people may be at a different place."

CELEBRATE MORE TIME WITH GOD

Teale said most clearly what many other women mentioned. "When he's away, I have more time for prayer and personal Bible study. When my husband is at home, we always put the kids to bed and then sit up and talk together. When he's gone, I have an hour or more for quiet time. I also depend on God more consciously, too."

CELEBRATE TIME TO PLUMB YOUR OWN DEPTHS

Mystery writer Nancy Pickard and I spent part of an afternoon together as I was researching this book. Pickard, divorced, said something so profound I grabbed an old envelope and scribbled furiously. She said, "I feel that living alone is an important passage in any woman's growing up. We can avoid it for years, but most of us will have to live alone some time.

"I thought I knew about living alone. I married late, and my husband was away a good bit during our marriage. However, I constantly used props to avoid being alone. After our divorce, I learned there is a difference between physical and emotional aloneness. If you use props—books, music, television, your children, drugs, alcohol, friends, romantic relationships—to fill your time, you are still avoiding being alone.

"If you learn to sit with your aloneness, dive into it, live through the pain it can bring, and come out on the other side, you discover you are stronger than you ever imagined.

"I think that only when we truly know how to be alone can we find union with something bigger than ourselves. How can you know what it feels like to be united with God until you know what it feels like to be utterly alone?"

A WISE WOMAN KNOWS
Some women merely grow old.
Others grow up.

A FINAL WORD

Millions of women live alone in our society. Some have children, many do not; some are single, divorced, or widowed, while others are legally married but required by their husband's work to spend much of their time alone.

Living alone is a challenge for a woman. It requires decisions, repairs, payments, and judgments for which we are often poorly prepared. However, we can take comfort in the fact that we are capable of doing what is required. We can reach out to other women in similar circumstances, who are more than willing to offer a hand in return. And sometimes—some miserable yet also wonderful times—we discover just how utterly we can depend on God.

Suggested Further Reading

Convissor, Kate. *Young Widow: Learning to Live Again*. Grand Rapids: Zondervan, 1992. A personal story, with insights for all young widows.

Ginsburg, Genevieve Davis. *To Live Again: Rebuilding Your Life After You've Become a Widow*. Los Angeles: Jeremy P. Tarcher, Inc., 1987. Based on a good bit of research with personal anecdotes.

Friedman, Dr. Sonia. *On a Clear Day You Can See Yourself: Turning the Life You Have into the Life You Want.* New York: Little, Brown, and Company, 1991. Excellent motivational book to move women from passivity to actively pursuing their own goals.

Storr, Dr. Anthony. *Solitude: A Return to the Self.* New York: The Free Press, 1988. A celebration of solitude as one major path to personal growth.

Patricia Sprinkle also offers a seminar on this topic for interested congregations and organizations. For more information, please contact her at 15086 SW 113th Street, Miami, FL 33196. Phone 305/385-3818.

CHECKLISTS FOR WOMEN HOME ALONE

CHECKLIST 1: A WOMAN HOME ALONE PREPAREDNESS KIT

A woman home alone can reduce some of the hassles in her life! Simply make sure you have the following:

❏ Emergency phone numbers by the telephone: not merely police and fire, but friends to call if needed
❏ Phone numbers for reliable repair services
❏ Medical reference book for adults and children
❏ Good home maintenance guide
❏ First-aid essentials (see Checklist 2)
❏ First-aid pantry (see Checklist 3)
❏ File of important family financial papers (see Checklist 4)
❏ File of appliance manuals, warranties, and receipts
❏ Manual for each automobile
❏ Fire extinguisher and smoke detectors
❏ Working flashlight with batteries
❏ Basic tool kit (see Checklist 5)
❏ Basic auto maintenance supplies (see Checklist 7)

And do the following things:

❏ Locate water cutoffs and metal "T" or get one (see page 187).
❏ Locate electrical or fuse box, label each circuit (see page 187-188).
❏ Make a schedule of when regular lawn, house, and auto maintenance needs to be done (See Checklist 6).

CHECKLIST 2: FIRST-AID ESSENTIALS

A woman home alone needs these things in easy reach for medical emergencies:

❑ Home health care manual
❑ Thermometer
❑ Bandage strips in several sizes
❑ First-aid cream (Neosporin, triple antibiotic, etc.)
❑ Rubbing alcohol (to sterilize wounds, thermometer, etc.)
❑ Hydrogen peroxide (to kill germs)
❑ Gauze pads and adhesive tape
❑ Cold pack in freezer for sprains
❑ Ace bandage
❑ Moist heating pad for pulled or sore muscles
❑ Antihistamine (Benedryl, etc.) for insect stings
❑ Ipecac for poisonings
❑ Pain relievers (aspirin, Tylenol, Advil, etc.)
❑ Sweet oil for earaches
❑ Aloe plant in kitchen for burns
❑ Scarf or tourniquet

CHECKLIST 3: FIRST-AID PANTRY

In Florida we keep hurricane pantries each summer and fall. A woman home alone should always keep the following foods in stock to see her through a spell of isolated sickness:

❑ Bullion granules, especially chicken
❑ Wheat germ
❑ Canned or frozen fruits
❑ Fruit juices: low-sodium vegetable, cranberry, apple, grape
❑ Soups: chicken and rice, chicken noodle, ramen noodles
❑ Honey and lemon juice (for sore throat)
❑ Salt (for gargle)
❑ Clear carbonated drinks (ginger ale, club soda, etc.)
❑ Frozen dinners
❑ Vitamins with minerals
❑ A few favorite, "splurgy" foods (to pamper yourself)

CHECKLIST 4: IMPORTANT FINANCIAL PAPERS TO KEEP

Papers to keep handy at home:

❑ Tax returns for the past seven years, including W–2 forms
❑ Brokerage account statements and bank statements
❑ Insurance policies
❑ Copies of wills (leave the original with lawyer or keep in a safety deposit box)
❑ Inventory of valuable possessions
❑ Number for each credit card and account numbers in case cards are stolen
❑ A record of all financial matters
❑ Social Security numbers for each family member (with a copy in your wallet)
❑ Car titles, registrations, and insurance papers

For the Safety Deposit Box (with copies at home for quick reference):

❑ Deeds
❑ IOU's
❑ Leases
❑ Stock certificates (may leave with broker)
❑ Marriage license, divorce papers, death certificates
❑ Birth certificates for each family member
❑ Original of will (may leave with lawyer)

CHECKLIST 5: A BASIC TOOL KIT

❏ *Hammer.* A 13 oz. hammer is a good weight for most women.

❏ *Screwdrivers* in several sizes, both straight blade and Phillips head, used for screws with holes like a cross.

❏ *Tape Measure.* Get a flexible steel one, ten to twelve feet long, that rolls back up by itself. The best ones have nail and screw sizes printed on the back. A one-inch width is easier to use than narrower ones—they bend too easily.

❏ *Razor knife.* A retractable safety one. Break off the blade each time it gets dull. Use to cut electrical and other tapes, finish wallpaper edges, and many other things.

❏ *Safety razor blades* with one protected edge. Use to scrape paint off windows and extra caulk off tubs.

❏ *Powerful flashlight.* Krypton bulbs are brighter, rechargeable batteries less expensive in the long run. We have one that stays plugged in when not in use, so we can find it.

❏ *Assorted nails and screws.*

❏ *Trouble light and sturdy extension cord* to check out problems in attics, crawl spaces, or in rooms where the power is out.

❏ *Plumber's plunger.* Large funnel-cups are best, because they create a stronger suction. Some people buy two, for sinks and toilets.

❏ *Carpenter's level.* Long tool shaped like a 2 x 4, with a small inset vial filled with liquid and a large air bubble. When held level, the bubble floats to the center. Used to hang things straight, establish a straight edge for a first piece of wallpaper, determine if a stove or washer needs to be leveled.

❏ *Adjustable wrench.* Get at least a 6-inch, to tighten and loosen bolts, especially on toilets and lavatories. If you get a 10-inch wrench too, you can hold with one while you turn the other.

❏ *Pliers.* For gripping, turning, and pulling.

❏ *Needle-nose pliers.* Handy for small items.

❏ *Drill and bits.* 3/8" variable-speed is most useful to hang pictures and plant hooks or, if cordless, to drain ceilings where leaks settle.

❏ *Putty knife.* A broad blunt blade with a handle, used to repair cracks and nail holes. Come in several widths. One inch is handiest.

Also Keep on Hand

❏ *Bathroom caulk*. To caulk tubs, sinks, etc. Elmer's has it in the same kind of bottle as Elmer's glue, easy to use.

❏ *Electrical tape*. Black and sticky. To repair nicked cords.

❏ *Long-stemmed matches* if your gas furnace or hot water heater has a pilot light.

❏ *Sandpaper* in several grades, especially extra fine, to smooth rough places on newly repaired walls or furniture.

❏ *Spackling compound*. To repair nail holes, gouges, wall cracks.

❏ *WD–40*. To loosen things you can't unscrew, or fix squeaky doors. Has many other uses, too! Read the label. My son used it on a computer keyboard that had been through a flood and got it working again.

CHECKLIST 6: HOME AND CAR MAINTENANCE SCHEDULE

General

Monthly:

❑ Change air filters in heating/air conditioning.
❑ Check automobile fluids.

Spring:

❑ Change smoke detector batteries.
❑ Check fire extinguishers.
❑ Check gutters, roof, downspouts.
❑ Have air conditioner checked.
❑ Check coolant in automobiles.
❑ Clean the chimney while soot is soft.

Late Summer:

❑ Get furnace checked.

Fall:

❑ Change smoke detector batteries.
❑ Check fire extinguishers.
❑ Check antifreeze in automobiles.
❑ Check snow tires (if you have snow).
❑ Clean leaves from gutters.
❑ Shut off outside water if in a freeze zone.

Personal

Jot down dates based on your own climate/situation.

❑ Fertilize lawn.
❑ Fertilize trees.
❑ Fertilize shrubs.
❑ Transplant flowers or trees.
❑ Change oil.
❑ Rotate tires.
❑ Buy license tags and get auto inspections.
❑ Other: _____

CHECKLIST 7: BASIC CAR SUPPLIES AND EQUIPMENT

Keep in car:

❑ map
❑ proof of insurance
❑ photocopy of car registration
❑ insurance number to call in case of emergency
❑ vehicle manual
❑ jumper cables to start a dead battery
❑ flares
❑ tire gauge
❑ jack, spare tire, and lug wrench
❑ spare quart of oil
❑ gallon plastic jug to carry water

Keep in garage or shed:

❑ oil in proper weight
❑ coolant
❑ windshield washer fluid

CHECKLIST 8: NEW HOME INSPECTION GUIDE

If you are seriously considering making an offer on a house, go through it with the owner, making notes and asking the following questions:

❑ *Rooms*. Measure each room, drawing as accurate a floor plan as you can to judge whether your furniture will fit. Look at the light in the house. Sunny houses lift spirits, dark houses dampen them. Ask:

- Which appliances and "fittings"—rugs, curtains, lights, fans—will be left?
- How old are the appliances?
- Are manuals available?
- Do fireplaces work? When were chimneys last swept?

❑ *Air conditioners and heating units:* Have them turned on. Note whether the blower is quiet. Ask:

- When were they last serviced?
- When were they installed?
- Do you have a service contract? With whom?

❑ *Wiring:* Check exposed wires for nicks and breaks. Note whether there are enough electrical outlets. Ask:

- When was wiring last done?
- Where is the electrical box?

❑ *Plumbing:* Check fixtures for cracks. Flush toilets, turn on all faucets to check flow and drainage. Check near plumbing for leaks or rotten wood that shows it has leaked. Rust on the water heater means it may need replacing soon.

❑ *Doors and windows:* Do they fit snugly? Do they open smoothly?

❑ *Floors and walls:* Are floors even and sturdy? Are walls free from large cracks?

❑ *Attic and basement:* Do exposed beams and joists appear sound? Is the attic well insulated? Look for dampness, rotten wood, sagging floors, and large cracks in the walls that indicate foundation shifts.

❑ *Paperwork:* Ask to see several months' utility bills to get some idea of what living costs will run. Ask to see a tax bill from last year. Also ask to see the tax assessment (for tax valuation) and compare with the appraisal of a professional appraiser hired by the seller.

❑ *Outside:* Ask for a layout or verbal description of plants not showing at that season, to avoid digging up something you'd later regret. Note whether large trees and shrubs appear healthy, and if sidewalks and driveways are in good condition. Look for damp spots near the house. Note whether the paint, roof shingles, gutters, and downspouts are in good condition. Also look for foundation wall cracks more than 1/4 inch wide. They may indicate that the house is settling.

❑ *Community:* Visit the street at different times of day. Listen for barking dogs or noisy children. Do people you see on the street look like congenial neighbors? Shop a couple of times in local markets. If you have children, visit district schools or ask the school board for standard scores for neighborhood schools, to compare with scores from other area schools. Higher test scores may indicate better teaching or more parent involvement in the schools.

MEET THE WOMEN
WHO SHARED

ALLISON is the busy mother of two elementary school sons and a preschool daughter. While her husband, a sales representative, covers a territory of several states, Allison busies herself with her Episcopal church's many programs.

AUGUST is married to a Coast Guard pilot who, when she was interviewed, was making frequent two-week trips while she was at home with their four young children. She later wrote happily, "He doesn't travel so much now." They are involved in an Assembly of God church.

BRENDA is married to a lawyer who was formerly employed by Prison Fellowship, traveling nationwide to work with states on criminal justice and retribution issues. Currently he works with the justice system on the island of Malta. After years as a professional woman, Brenda is now at home with their preschool son.

DIANE is single and employed as a recreation therapist for a state mental health hospital. She is involved in a Presbyterian congregation, choir, and children's ministry.

DOREEN is divorced, has two grown sons, and teaches special education. She is very active in the Quota Club and attends an Evangelical Covenant church.

DOT had been widowed for seven years when interviewed, and has a married daughter. After her husband died, she took a job as a food product representative. Recently she relocated to be near her family. Her friends and Presbyterian congregation miss her!

FRANCES is a retired elementary teacher and a widow. She is active in the United Methodist Church, and a member of

Christian Women's Fellowship. She is also my special, supportive mother-in-law.

JAYNE is divorced, has two grown children, and lives alone. She is a guidance counselor at a junior high school and is active in a Presbyterian church.

JEAN, married thirty years, has three grown children. Her husband is both a lawyer and a state legislator, so must be in the state capitol for a sixty-day session each year. Committee work and legal responsibilities take him away from home approximately 15–20 percent of the rest of the time. Jean sometimes travels with him, but is about to begin a career as a director of relocation for a real estate broker. They are active in a Presbyterian church.

JILL is the wife of a Christian publishing executive whose work requires him to travel approximately 25 percent of the month. They have three children, ages eleven to seventeen. Jill's situation as a woman home alone is complicated by the fact that she has Lupus.

JUDI was widowed at forty-five and has one son in boarding school. She got a master's degree after her husband died and began a career as a teacher "after playing tennis for twenty-five years." She is involved in an Episcopal church.

JUDY is married to a land appraiser for the Corps of Engineers whose work frequently takes him out of town for several days. They are active in The Rock, a charismatic congregation. She and her husband were the couple who first felt God calling me to write this book.

JUNE is married to a pilot and employed by a Christian service agency as coordinator of personnel and management information services. She has a teenage daughter.

KAREN is married to a retired Coast Guard Commander who, after retirement, worked for several months in a distant city and returned each weekend. Just as I finished this book he was offered a position that will require a family move, but very little traveling. The parents and three of their five children also have an extensive puppet ministry in their local Catholic church and community.

KEY is married to a Coast Guard officer. In their first fifteen years of marriage he spent the equivalent of seven years away on various cruises. They have two preschool children and Key, a CPA, works at home. They have relocated since our interview, but wherever they live, Key's church is important to her.

LAUREN's husband is in the Air National Guard, which takes him out of town two weeks twice a year and one evening a week; in addition, he is a boat broker and attends boat shows many weekends. They have one preschool son. Lauren keeps the books for her father's automobile dealership and is active in a Presbyterian church.

LORI is married to a Naval pilot and has an infant daughter. Soon after our interview he was transferred to the NATO base in Italy, where the family now lives. She wrote, "It is beautiful, but once again I am alone a great deal! I do plan on taking advantage of this fantastic opportunity to travel, and the community here is quite supportive."

LYNN is married to Bas Vanderzalm, International Director for World Relief, whose position requires him to be away from home approximately 25 percent of the time. Overseas trips typically require three to four weeks. They have two children, and Lynn and her daughter both have chronic fatigue syndrome. Lynn is also the author of *Finding Strength in Weakness: Help and Hope for Families Battling Chronic Fatigue Syndrome* (Grand Rapids: Zondervan, 1995).

MARTHA is the mother of two teenage girls, and is married to a salesman who flies out most Mondays and returns on Thursdays. She is a homemaker, and initiated and now organizes an annual March for Jesus in her city. Their family is active in a local Episcopal church.

NANCY PICKARD is divorced, the mother of one son, and the creator of the Jenny Cain mystery series, which has won major mystery awards. Her "interview" was a serendipity that happened while we were driving back from a cup of coffee and signing books at a local bookstore. Her newest mystery is *Twilight* (New York: Pocketbooks, 1995).

PAULA, single, is an accountant for a print solutions manufacturer. Soon after our interview she bought her first home. She is currently active in a Baptist congregation. As the pianist in our former church, she was the woman home alone who started this whole book!

PRISCILLA was formerly married to a man who worked on an off-shore oil rig, and they have two sons. After her divorce she lived alone, but each son returned to her for his senior year. She is employed as the finance secretary of a large Episcopal congregation. She attends The Rock, a charismatic congregation.

SARAH GAY is single, teaches high school Latin, and is an elder in the Presbyterian church. During summers she frequently takes interesting vacations, such as to rain forests in Costa Rica or a bicycle tour of rural Delaware.

SUE has been married to a Coast Guard Captain for twenty-one years; he'd been stationed on ships six years of that. They have two teenagers and one preschooler, and until the last baby was born, Sue taught piano. They are involved in a Lutheran church.

SUSAN is a middle school teacher, mother of a married son and teenage daughter, and married to a man whose work currently takes him out of town about 50 percent of the time. Their family actively attends a Calvary Chapel and is very supportive of Navigator Ministries.

SUZANNE, when interviewed, was the mother of an active four-year-old son, expecting her second child soon, and recovering from a sprained ankle. Her husband traveled in automotive sales and was gone each week. After the birth of their daughter, her husband received a promotion and the family moved. She wrote: "Now he works long hours at the office, but that's OK. He's not on the road anymore!"

TEALE teaches in a Christian school. She is married to an executive staff member with an international missions organization, and they have three sons. They are active in a local charismatic congregation.

NOTES

Chapter One: *Millions of Courageous Women*

1. 1990 U.S. census data reported in Robert Famighetti, ed., *The World Almanac and Book of Facts 1994* (Mahwah, NJ: Funk & Wagnalls, 1993), 960–61.

2. Barbara Holland, *One's Company: Reflections on Living Alone* (New York: Ballantine, 1992), 14.

3. Dana Treen, "A Family of One: Singles Suffer Social, Workplace Slights," *Florida Times Union*, 7 February 1994, sec. B, p. 1.

Chapter Two: *In the Valley of Decision*

1. Ruth A. Tucker, *Multiple Choices: Making Wise Decisions in a Complicated World* (Grand Rapids: Zondervan, 1992), 77. Used by permission of Zondervan Publishing House.

2. Ruth Tucker, 23.

3. Ruth Tucker, 24, 74.

4. Genevieve Davis Ginsberg, *To Live Again: Rebuilding Your Life After You've Become a Widow* (Los Angeles: Jeremy P. Tarcher, 1987), 35.

Chapter Three: *Keeping Worries Down to Size*

1. Adam Phillips, "A Psychoanalysis of Worry," *Harper's* 286 (April 1993): 29.

Chapter Four: *Even My Shadow Is Lonely*

1. Barbara Holland, 6.

2. Charles Fracchia, *How to Be Single Creatively* (New York: McGraw-Hill, 1979), 52.

3. Anthony Storr, *Solitude: A Return to the Self* (New York: The Free Press, 1988), 28.

4. Elisabeth Elliot, *The Path of Loneliness* (Nashville: Thomas Nelson, 1988), 127.

5. Dr. Sonya Friedman with Guy Kettlehack, *On a Clear Day You Can See Yourself* (New York: Little, Brown and Company, 1991), 62.

6. Charles Fracchia, 6–7.

7. Penelope Russianoff, *Why Do I Think I Am Nothing Without a Man?* (New York: Bantam, 1982), 89.

8. Lorraine O'Connell, "Life with a Loner: It's Important to Have a Sense of Your Own Self," *The Washington Post*, 20 May 1994, sec. C, p. 5.

9. Barbara Holland, 15.

10. Penelope Russianoff, 82.

11. Meg Woodson, *Making It Through the Toughest Days of Grief* (Grand Rapids: Zondervan, 1994), 54. Used by permission of Zondervan Publishing House.

12. Elisabeth Elliot, 22.

Chapter Five: *Home for the Holidays—Alone*

1. Meg Woodson, 12–13.

2. Evan Imber-Black and Janine Roberts, "Family Change: Don't Cancel Holidays!" *Psychology Today* 26 (March-April 1993): 62–65. See also Evan Imber-Black and Janine Roberts, *Rituals for Our Times* (New York: HarperCollins, 1992).

3. Imber-Black and Roberts, 62.

Chapter Seven: *When Aspirins Aren't Enough*

1. Charles Strouse, "Poll: Seniors Worry about Crime, Illness," *The Miami Herald*, 2 December 1994, sec. B, p. 1.

2. Lisa Delaney, "Awaken the Doctor Within: How You Can Take Full Advantage of Your Inner Powers of Healing," *Prevention* (October 1993): 60.

3. Lisa Delaney, 132.

Chapter Eight: *Things That Go Bump in the Night*

1. Barbara Holland, 223.

2. Gwen and Don Carden with Police Commander Sadie Darnell, *Protect Yourself From Crime* (Boca Raton: Globe Communications Corp., 1993), 4.

3. *Newsweek*, 21 March 1994, 71.

4. Barbara Holland, 223.

5. George MacDonald, *Diary of An Old Soul* (Minneapolis: Augsberg, 1975), 10.

Chapter Eleven: *Staying Safe in Public Places*

1. Quoted by Gwen and Don Carden with Police Commander Sadie Darnell, 13.

2. Peter Martin Commanday, "Practical Peacemaking for Educators: Your Personal Safety," *Education Digest* 58 (May 1993): 15.

Chapter Twelve: *Staying Safe Around Other People*

1. While these tips come from several places, many are from Dr. Elizabeth Davis, quoted by Gwen and Don Carden with Police Commander Sadie Darnell, 18–19.

2. Judith A. H. Luchsinger, *Practical Self-Defense for Women: A Manual of Prevention and Escape Techniques* (Minneapolis: Dillon Press, 1977), 13.

3. Sonya Martinez, "Scared No More: One Girl's Story," *Seventeen* 52 (October 1993): 50.

Chapter Thirteen: *What To Do If You Are the Victim of a Crime*

1. Bruce Tegner and Alice McGrath, *Self-Defense and Assault Prevention for Girls and Women: A Physical Education Course* (New York: Thor, 1977), 60.

Chapter Fourteen: *Watch Out for People Traps!*

1. Dr. Henry Cloud and Dr. John Townsend, *Safe People* (Grand Rapids: Zondervan, 1995), 11. Used by permission of Zondervan Publishing House.

2. Cloud and Townsend, 41–60.

3. Anthony Storr, xiii.

4. Barbara Holland, 20.

5. Meg Woodson, 120.

Chapter Sixteen: *Alone—With Two Children, Three Gerbils, and a Dog*

    1. Patricia Sprinkle, *Do I Have To? What to Do About Children Who Do Too Little Around the House* (Grand Rapids: Zondervan, 1993), 67.

    2. Patricia Sprinkle, 43–44.

    3. Anthony Storr, 32.

Chapter Seventeen: *When the Children Are Sick*

    1. *Boy Scout Handbook*, Tenth Edition, Irving, TX: Boy Scouts of America, 1990, 405–17.

    2. Sandra Jacobs, "How Sick is SICK?" *The Miami Herald*, 21 October 1994, sec. F, p. 1

Chapter Eighteen: *Families Where Dad Comes and Goes*

    1. This anecdote by Todd Schneckloth appeared in "Life in These United States," *Reader's Digest*, October 1994, 90. Copyright © 1994 by the Reader's Digest Association. (Permission secured.)

Chapter Nineteen: *Basic Finances Any Woman Needs To Know*

    1. Mary Lynne McDonald, *The Christian's Guide to Money Matters for Women* (Grand Rapids: Zondervan, 1995), 8.

    2. Lois G. Forer, *What Every Woman Needs to Know Before (and After) She Gets Involved with Men and Money* (New York: Rawson Associates, 1993), 21.

    3. Penelope Russianoff, 136.

Chapter Twenty-One: *Planning for the Future*

    1. Claire McIntosh, "The B.E. Guide to Easy, No-Nonsense Financial Planning," *Black Enterprise*, October 1993, 112.

    2. Claire McIntosh, 115.

    3. Penelope Russianoff, 135.

    4. Gary D. Moore, *The Thoughtful Christian's Guide to Investing* (Grand Rapids: Zondervan, 1990), 235. Used by permission of Zondervan Publishing House.

    5. Gary D. Moore, 96.

    6. Gary D. Moore, 63.

    7. Lynn Caine, *Widow* (New York: William Morrow, 1974), 159.

Chapter Twenty-Two: *Money Questions to Ask Before You Marry*

    1. Shelby White, *What Every Woman Should Know About Her Husband's Money* (New York: Turtle Bay Books, 1992), 27.

    2. Lois G. Forer, 31.

Chapter Twenty-Three: *What a Wife Home Alone Also Needs to Know About Money*

    1. Lynn Caine, 152.

    2. Three statistics from Shelby White, 238.

    3. Lois Forer, 15.

    4. Ruth Tucker, 114.

    5. Shelby White, 27.

    6. Shelby White, 223.

    7. Ruth Tucker, 115.

Chapter Twenty-Four: *What to Do Before You Have an Emergency*

    1. Lyn Herrick, *Anything He Can Fix, I Can Fix Better* (Valle Crucis, NC: Quality Living Publications, 1990), 2.

Chapter Twenty-Seven: *How to Get the Help You Need*

    1. Kate Convissor, *Young Widow: Learning to Live Again* (Grand Rapids: Zondervan, 1992), 80.

    2. Caroline Bird, *Lives of Our Own: Secrets of Salty Old Women* (Boston: Houghton Mifflin, 1995), 1.

    3. Charles Fracchia, 5.